Raven
Transcending
Fear

By Terri Kozlowski

Higher Ground Books & Media
Springfield, Ohio.
http://www.highergroundbooksandmedia.com

Printed in the United States of America 2021

Dedication

I dedicate this book to all those, like myself, who suffered childhood traumas that are inconceivable for our immature minds to comprehend. I hope the retelling of my story gives you the courage to embark on your own healing journey. One that transcends the fear and returns you to your authentic self. Back to the realization that you're worthy and have limitless potential.

Preface

The memoir before you is my story from my perspective. My truth as I experienced it. It may not be how others in my life experienced or remember the same events. I am writing without negative feelings nor resentments of those portrayed in this memoir.

We are born into a family. Some people enter our lives for periods of time and others that leave; it is how this Earth school works. Each person I have come in contact with I have learned something from, so I am thankful for their part in my story.

Introduction

The raven has significant meaning to me since I discovered my Native American roots. My mother came from the Raven Clan of the Tlingit tribe of Athabascan Indians in Alaska. Although she would say she was proud of her heritage, she didn't teach me about the traditions or our legacy. I had to learn about it on my own.

When in high school, I researched ravens in the library. I was surprised to learn they are as intelligent as dolphins and chimpanzees. They use tools, can mimic the sounds of other animals, and are incredibly adaptable to whatever their surroundings provide. They are also very curious and confident, which can come across as mischievous as they are also playful. The birds mate for life and are capable of empathy. As I learned more about them, I became more intrigued, especially the symbolism that they imputed.

The all-black raven is most often linked with death and loss, so it's seen as a negative warning. However, the raven is merely connecting this world to the spirit world. In the Bible, they are an example of God's provision for the world. Greek mythology shows them associated with light and wisdom. In African cultures, they are a guide. In Asia, they are messengers of the gods. Within Norse mythology, the raven symbolizes the mind and intelligence.

Even Dr. Carl Jung, famed psychologist, used the raven as a symbol of the shadow self, our darker side. But he also saw that the raven symbolism was showing the balance between light and dark through wisdom. By allowing ourselves to look at the shadows, we enable secrets to be exposed to the light of our consciousness. This insight into the raven's characteristics and symbolism intrigued me.

Then I discovered what the raven meant to my Tlingit heritage. It's the creator, responsible for bringing about creation as well as bringing the light to this dark world. It also is the messenger for us to the spirit world. So, it's a creature of metamorphosis, symbolizing transformation. The raven inspires us to look within to seek answers, but with the knowledge, we can soar high over the obstacles that we encounter so that we can grow.

This knowledge empowered a part of me to begin a journey that I didn't want to take. I was so overcome with fear after a fateful trip to New Mexico, and I didn't know how to return to myself. But the magic of the Raven Clan and its ability to communicate mysteries and give clarity to thoughts encouraged me to take steps that I needed toward transformation.

What my physical eyes see is not necessarily the truth. Through the raven's magical shapeshifting abilities, I could tear down the world my egoic mind built to entrap me and rebuild the life I came here to live. This transformation out of pain and darkness to light was a healing process. I gained the courage I needed to look at myself with introspection. Through the rebirth out of fear, I learned to honor my ancestors, remember how to play, enjoy life, and see the magic all around me. My change of consciousness opened me up to new growth, self-knowledge, and creative powers that were always inside me. Those things about myself that I had forgotten because of trauma.

Those of us who have been through horrible ordeals can all claim the same heritage of the Raven Clan because it's the story of humanity. It's the tale of how we can rediscover our authentic self and return to the love that we are all seeking.

CHAPTER 1 WHO WE TRULY ARE

CHILDREN ARE BORN UNAFRAID

Raven; the bringer of light

~Intelligent

~Wise

~Persuasive

~Calm

Knowing its purpose;

Confident and ready.

As all children are, I was born unafraid. I came into this world, knowing that I am a being of light. I understood that I am worthy. I recognized that I am here to love and be loved. I came knowing what I am supposed to do. Aware of my full potential. Confident and ready to fulfill my purpose. Moving forward into the unknown without fear; fear is a learned behavior. This unknown shaped me. The family I was born into in November 1968, is the first unknown I encountered.

Born into this Earth school, my parents give me a name — Terri Marie. They give me a religion — Lutheran. I am born with an ethnicity into a family that has its own set of baggage that they inadvertently pass on to me. This new family told me who I am, not necessarily allowing me to develop as God intended, as a human being of love.

Seeing pictures of myself taken when I was little, I see a spunky, carefree individual whose light is so bright I glow. There's a glint in my eye and a big smile on my round chubby face. The little girl I see in the picture is ready to take on the world, with confidence and fearlessness. I know where I'm going and what I intend to do with my life.

For my grandmother's upcoming birthday, my dad, a professional photographer, took me to his studio to take some pictures of me. With the lights shining down on my brilliant yellow dress, he claimed that I intently watched him the entire time he photographed me. He didn't pose me in any way; he believed in natural shots of me just being me. He says that during this photoshoot, I carefully scrutinized what he was doing and how he was doing it. The looks and expressions I gave him were silent messages; messages that he wasn't doing it correctly. My eyes told him volumes of information — mainly that he should listen to what I had to say, despite not being able to converse. I always seemed to have an answer, even if I wasn't asked a question. He declares that one day, I went from being his little girl to being a 40-year-old woman, instantaneously.

My paternal grandmother told an amusing story that illustrates my self-determined nature. When I was just two-and-a-half years old, my mother put me and my litter sister, Tammi, down for a nap and made a phone call in the other room of our apartment. I wasn't sleepy—I was hungry, and I wanted a snack. My sister was sound asleep in her crib, so I got out of bed. I put on my rubber galoshes with no socks and headed down the steep flight of steps to my grandmother's apartment. My grandparents owned the apartment building on Clay Avenue in downtown Jeannette, a small town in Western Pennsylvania.

When I got down the steps, I went looking for my grandmother. I looked in the kitchen where she usually was, but couldn't find her. I searched in her bedroom, but she wasn't there either. I searched behind the large wooden doors of the sitting room, but I still didn't find her. So, I headed down another very steep set of stairs, through the first heavy door to the foyer. Another heavy door and a few more steps, and I had made it out to the busy main street of town.

I walked with determination about a block down the street all by myself to Duncan Hardware, the store that my grandparents owned. I stood outside, looking through the large, hefty glass door of the shop as it was too heavy for me to open. The clerks inside recognized me and opened the door to let me in. It was an ample supply store that smelled like oil and wood. It had tall ladders on wheels that moved back and forth, so the clerks could climb up to get items for the customers. I walked straight to the back of the building. I went right past my grandfather, directly past the penny nail display that I loved to play in, to where my grandmother's office was—she was the bookkeeper for the store. I marched right up to her, very confidently, and asked for a cookie for the doll I had brought with me on my venture. Grandma described me as a very independent and fearless little girl.

My parents met while my dad was based at Fort Lewis Army base in Washington State before leaving for his three-year tour in Vietnam. Daddy was born in Western Pennsylvania, from a typical loving family of that era. A slender man with brown wavy hair, intrigued by science, he also had a creative side. He believed in duty, honor, and serving his country. He enlisted in the army so that he could choose his MOS (Military Occupational Specialty); the job he wanted to have was a photographer. He informed me that he married my mother before shipping out so someone would receive his death benefit, as he didn't believe he'd survive the war. He almost didn't.

If he tells the story, which I only ever heard once, it's with little emotion, just the facts. While taking photographs from a helicopter that was flying over the jungle, the Huey was suddenly under attack. The gunner was the first to be killed; my dad grabbed the gun and began firing at the terrain below. The Huey's tail rotor was shot and destroyed, which caused the helicopter to do a tailspin as it smashed into the ground. The crew was missing in action for three days before my dad, the only survivor, was found. The crash broke his back, which has caused him great pain throughout the years.

My mother had a completely different and harrowing history. She is an Athabascan Indian, Gwich'in tribe, Raven Clan, from Fort Yukon Alaska—eight miles inside the Arctic Circle. She spent the first sixteen years of her life as the eldest daughter in this very harsh environment before her mom, a widow with 16 children, gave the three oldest girls up for adoption. She left everything she had known and entered what she called the "white man's world." She and her sisters hadn't ever seen running water or electricity. She told me they spent their first night watching the toilet water go down when it was flushed and playing with the light switch—on ... off ... on ... off ... on ... off.

In the late fall of 1970, my dad re-enlisted in the army. He was stationed at the 130th General Hospital in Nuremberg, Germany. We moved into a small apartment on Oskar-von-Miller-Strauss near the Dozen Lakes, where we would take walks and feed the ducks. We weren't there too long because I decided to catch my sister's crib on fire and the landlord didn't like that very much.

My parents smoked, as did many people in this era, before they knew that the habit was slowly killing them or how addictive nicotine was. My dad had a gleaming, silver-tone, Zippo lighter, the kind that when you opened the lid, it automatically had a flame. I used to watch him open it, and a little flame appeared for him to light his or my mother's cigarette. It was always in his pocket except when he went to bed; then, it was on his nightstand.

I had a big girl bed, and my sister slept in a crib in the nursery. It was a large room with a rocking chair, a toy box, and a glass panel in the door so my parents could check on us when we were napping. One quiet Sunday morning, I went to see if my parents were awake so one of them could get Tammi out of the crib. We wanted to play, but both of them were sound asleep and did not hear me come into the room. There on the nightstand, sparkling in the early sunlight, was the silver lighter. I had never held it before. It was cold to the touch. I took it back to the nursery to show Tammi. I shut the door and went over to the crib and opened the Zippo so Tammi could see the flame. Open, close … open, close … open, close. As I kept playing with it, the metal of the lighter casing heated up enough that I burnt my hand and dropped the lighter into Tammi's crib—while it was open.

It's incredible how quickly the crib bedding caught fire. Tammi started crying, and I seriously struggled to pull her out of the crib before it was aflame. We hid behind the rocking chair and were screaming—not for my parents to come but for Heidi, our little chocolate dachshund, to get out from under the crib where she slept. It got so hot in the nursery that the glass panel in the door shattered, which woke my parents.

My dad came running into the room in his underwear and bare feet, saw the flames, and grabbed the fire extinguisher that was in the hallway to put out the fire. Tammi and I were still screaming for Heidi, so my dad crawled under the crib to get her. We were all scared, but okay; my dad had the only injury — cut up feet from walking on the broken glass panel from the nursery door. Soon after the fire, we moved to the high-rise apartment building in Nuremberg.

Mom, Tammi, and I were off to the basement of our new home to wash some clothes in the laundry facilities. I noticed that mom wasn't paying attention to us as Tammi and I went to the hallway where the elevator was to play. Another resident came down off of the elevator to do her laundry, so Tammi and I went through the open doors. It was astounding that the wall panel had so many buttons on it! When you pushed the buttons, they lit up! So we, of course, pushed every button we could. Neither of us noticed that the elevator doors closed, or that we were moving. We did see when the elevator stopped, but the doors didn't open. It seems we caused the lift to stop between floors and we were stuck.

I am not sure when mom realized we were missing, but it took a couple of hours before the elevator started to move again. When the doors did open, we were greeted by firemen in big boots and coats, carrying axes — a little scary, especially when we heard my mother crying. Once Tammi heard her, she was crying too. She ran to my mother; I calmly went over to the fireman to inform him that the buttons on the panel wouldn't light up anymore. Pragmatic, I always seemed to stay calm when unexpected events occurred.

The Christkindl Market in Nuremberg is well-known for its vendors' high-quality products, food, holiday cheer, and for being the ideal place for families to gather as part of their holiday traditions. The one thing I remember most about the market was the smell. An odd mixture of stale beer, sweet pastries, and bratwurst all combined — thinking about it still makes me nauseous.

One sunny winter day, my mother, Tammi, and I were on our way to the Christkindl market via the cable car system that went throughout the city. We liked the trolley. This time of year, it was fun looking out the windows and seeing all the incredible Christmas decorations and large window displays the stores had for the holiday season.

As we approached the market, my mother rose and told me to head for the exit. When we stopped, and the door opened, I stepped onto the cobbled stone street. My mother was behind me. The trolley door shut, and it started to move away when I realized that Tammi didn't get off the streetcar. I began to scream Tammi's name. My mother seemed confused and looked around the street to see if Tammi wandered off. I started to chase the trolley as it was moving away, screaming for Tammi. A short distance away, it stopped, and the doors opened. When I got up to the streetcar, Tammi was standing in the doorway sobbing. I took her hand and got her onto the street when my mother realized what had happened and started to approach us. I was calming Tammi as my mother started to scold her for not getting off the trolley with us. After this event, I began to hold Tammi's hand when we were out. I became responsible for my little sister, as I felt that my mother needed help in this area.

Our final apartment in Germany was in the countryside. My dad was able to have a garden near the cellar, where he planted what he thought were pretty yellow flowers, based on the picture of the seed packet. He planted them against the wall, and they grew rather tall. When they started to form seeds in the center, he realized they were huge sunflowers. Tammi was horrified by the garden because these flowers were always looking down on her in a foreboding way. Yet, for me, they were happy flowers.

I was not too fond of the garden because of the daddy-long-legs. I like spiders; I will catch them if found in the house and set them free. They will eat the bugs I don't like; mosquitos, flies, and the like. Daddy-long-leg spiders were creepy to my four-year-old self, and the garden seemed to be full of them. Their extremely long legs were strange, and they shook their webs as a defense mechanism. My dad caught one to show us that they cannot hurt us. He said that they are poisonous, but that their fangs are too small to bite us; the spiders were safe. Years later, I found out that this story about the daddy-long-leg being poisonous wasn't right, just folklore, but for now, I was no longer afraid of the daddy-long-leg and helped my dad weed the garden.

Being in the country meant there were a lot of farms around. There was a chain-link fence between the apartment building and a massive cornfield. The fence wasn't secured to the ground in some spots due to the landscape of the area. At one place in the fence, we could crawl under to get into the cornfield. Tammi and I, with the other neighbor kids, would play tag and hide-n-seek amongst the stalks of tall corn. As evening approached one summer day, we were all heading back home after playing in the cornfield when Tammi got stuck under the fence. We tried to free her by holding up the barrier so she could get through but to no avail. I decided we needed an adult to help, but no one wanted to get in trouble for being on the other side of the fence. Tammi was crying and became more upset when I told her I had to get daddy. She didn't want me to leave her there, and the other kids didn't want to stay and get in trouble. After taking a few minutes to calm her down and assuring her I would be back with help, she let me go.

I ran back home and told my dad that Tammi was under the fence and couldn't get out. At that moment, he didn't ask any questions. He just ran back outside with me to Tammi. When we got to her, she was trying to wiggle out from underneath the tight barrier. I giggled when I saw her, as she was flailing under the fence, trying to free herself. Once I started laughing, so did Tammi, which made it more difficult for my dad to free her from the fencing. When we calmed down, my dad moved the fence, and I pulled Tammi out. From an early age, I was able to problem solve as well as know when I needed help; and wasn't afraid to ask for it.

Four families total lived in the small complex in the country; an Italian family, an English family, a German family, and us. All the families had children, and we all played together. At first, it was challenging to communicate, but children are intelligent and innovative. We created our own jargon, with a mixture of words from each of the languages so that we could talk with one another.

Once we got back to the States, my sister and I still used this language with each other. My dad got concerned about this. He asked one of the pediatricians he worked with at the Uniformed Services University of the Health Sciences Hospital in Bethesda, Maryland, about it and was told not to worry. We would grow out of it when we got around other children who just spoke English. We did outgrow it. Children are born creative, and they're ingenious if they are allowed to be what God intended for them to be.

After our return to the States in 1974, we moved to a lovely townhouse on Yellow Rose Court in Columbia, Maryland. It was the first planned community in the U.S. In this home, Tammi and I had a playroom. There was a community play area for the children with a sandbox and swing set. There also was a creek that we used to go and play in during the summer. It was a happy place. My fondest childhood memories with my family occurred here.

My sister and I went to Phelps Luck Elementary school, which we walked to, one mile each way. As a planned community, Columbia had walking trails that we used to stroll on to get to school. Some mornings my mother came with us, but every afternoon we were alone for the return home. We had friends from the neighborhood that we would walk with some days, but Tammi and I always stayed together.

One afternoon I burst through the front door in tears. Some kids at school were calling me "chink-ka girl" because my eyes were slightly slanted, and they said I must be from China. Children aren't born disliking others; hate is a learned behavior. I was upset that they were calling me a name and that they didn't want to hear about where I was born. I wasn't crying because they were teasing me, but because they wouldn't listen to the truth.

My mother's reaction was unusual; she got furious. She threw the spatula in her hand at the wall. She started yelling about our Native American heritage, which, at this time, I knew very little about my culture. She was screaming about how the "White Man" came and took our land away, even though no one has the right to own the land of the Earth — it's a gift for us to be able to use. She ranted for several minutes before she realized I was whimpering in the corner, hugging Tammi. Being so caught up in her own feelings, she didn't make me feel any better. I felt that by sharing my hurt, I caused others pain.

I learned years later that her adoptive parents didn't allow my mom or her sisters to speak their native language, Athabascan. They weren't allowed to keep any of their customs, and all of the clothes and regalia they brought with them from Alaska were thrown away. Their heritage, who they were, and where they came from—all of this was taken away. My mother was emotionally reacting to her past and not directly to the name-calling that I suffered. When who we are is ripped from us, it's a hard road back to our authentic selves.

Tammi and I loved to play in the creek. We would catch tadpoles and put them in a bucket of water and watch them become frogs over the next few weeks before letting them go. We once had a turtle come to the back patio of the townhouse. Tammi and I were very excited and called daddy to see it. He, however, was not happy about the visitor. That day we learned what a snapping turtle was and how it could "snap" a twig thicker than my dad's finger in half before we could blink. It was horrifying, but we didn't get near any of the turtles in the creek anymore.

The creek wasn't very deep unless we had much rain. We would walk through it a good way to where it pooled a bit. In the summer, we would romp in the pooling water. Farther down the creek, it went under the road through a conduit, which seemed enormous. We weren't allowed to go into the pipe. You could hear the cars traveling across the bridge overhead; it scared Tammi. I used to go into it and sit against the concrete wall. I thought it was quiet, and since Tammi wouldn't come in, I was alone. Being alone didn't happen very often since we did everything together. Only eleven months apart, people thought we were twins. We had the same clothes, but wore different colors — I wore blue, and Tammi wore pink.

Because I saw that mom didn't always pay close attention to us, I felt that I had to take care of Tammi. This responsibility that I took on meant that we spent a lot of time together. But even at a young age, I knew that I needed my alone time; it's essential to my soul. So, the few minutes I stole in the conduit were valuable.

During our time in Maryland, when I was six years old, I was close to my mother. I helped her stir the macaroni and cheese while standing on a chair in our kitchen to help her make dinner. I learned to mix her drinks — vodka and whatever juice we had in the refrigerator. I cleaned up after she passed out on the couch, so my dad wouldn't find out. My mother was always drinking something from the special cabinet in the wall unit. I realized at a young age that her alcohol consumption wasn't typical.

As a person with epilepsy, my mother took phenobarbital and, when mixed with the liquor, it would induce seizures. Still, she continued to drink despite the known dangers. I recall one particular day when she fell on the powder room floor. Tammi started screaming, which was my cue to get the wooden spoon she used to beat us with and place it on her tongue until she stopped seizing. The first time I remember doing this, I was five years old. Children are so adaptive and obedient; I didn't realize that I was becoming co-dependent. Co-dependency is a relationship where one person has an addiction, and the other person is psychologically dependent on the first in an unhealthy way. For me, it showed up as a need to take care of my mother and my sister. To protect mom from getting into trouble with daddy because of her drinking, and to protect Tammi from my mother's inattention.

At seven years old, my parents separated. Essentially, my mom left. Tammi wanted to go with her, but I chose to stay with my dad. Her moving out was the first time that my sister and I were separated, and Tammi didn't understand why I didn't want to go with them. I told Tammi that someone needed to take care of daddy since she and mom would be together. My dad sued for full custody of my sister and me. He was the first man to win full guardianship of two small girls in the state of Maryland. I thought this was a solid win for him, but I found out later that my mother didn't show up to the hearing. She always told me that she "gave us" to my dad and, in her mind, I guess she did. I'm grateful for this outcome. When I look back over my life, I can see God's hand, even though I didn't feel His presence at times.

Tammi and I lived separately for two months. I continued to walk to and from school all by myself. My dad left the sliding glass door off the patio unlocked so I could get in when I got home from school. While I waited the three hours for him to come home, I would play, read, and watch television. One afternoon I got home, and the TV was gone. I called my dad on the green rotary phone that hung in the kitchen and asked if he took it to work with him. He said no. He told me that some special policemen would be coming to the house and that I was supposed to let them in. They were the FBI.

My dad's job with the army involved some special equipment, and they needed to verify that everything was all right. I was very excited to get my fingerprints taken; they had to be able to eliminate my prints from the robbers. I asked many questions, and I got to play with the fluffy brush to dust for fingerprints in unimportant areas of the house until my dad arrived. It seems that my mother told some of her friends who lived in the neighborhood how I would use the sliding glass door to get into the townhouse, and they stole the television. Children are born fearless, happy, and intuitive; they learn to fear, to think negatively, and to close off their instinctive selves based on their experiences. This incident was the beginning of me becoming aware that not everyone, including my mother, is trustworthy.

When school let out for the summer, Tammi and I went to visit my grandparents in Western Pennsylvania. We were very excited. They had moved from the small town to the country and had a three-foot above ground pool put in for us to swim. We quickly made friends with the next-door neighbor girls. And a homeless basset hound showed up at the beginning of our visit. The dog stayed for the summer, too. It was a beautiful and loving experience. We had to help clean the house every Saturday morning before we could play; Tammi and I would take turns dusting and vacuuming. We didn't have to make our own meals as we had done before; my grandmother prepared breakfast, lunch, and dinner each day. She read bedtime stories to us, and we prayed every night. She taught me about God. We both knew that she loved us and wanted us to be with her. When we stayed with my grandmother, things felt very different than how my mother handled our daily lives.

My dad got me a cat, which I named Betaline, and we had to leave her in Maryland when we went to visit my grandmother because she was allergic to cats. My dad would call each week to talk with Tammi and me, and he told me that he thought Beta was going to have kittens. I was very excited. Each week he would call, and I asked for a kitten update. One week he said Beta wasn't going to have any kittens; that sometimes, if the babies are sick, they go to heaven instead of being born. I'm not sure I quite understood, but my grandmother had us pray that Beta's kittens were happy with God. I liked that idea, even though I secretly wanted the kittens back.

When it was time to go back to school, we went back to the townhouse in Maryland to live with my dad. One chilly evening, my dad told me to get slippers on my cold feet, and I went up to my room and looked under my bed—and started screaming. My dad was right behind me so fast I bumped into him, holding a tiny fluffy kitten. It seemed that Beta had her kittens under my bed, unbeknownst to my dad. I was delighted. My dad wasn't; Beta was an indoor/ outdoor kitty, and her kittens had fleas. My dad spent the rest of the evening, bathing them to get rid of the pests. This instance was the first remembrance I had of God answering my prayers.

In the fall of 1977, when I turned nine, my parents' divorce proceedings started to get more intense, and my mother's drinking amplified. During Christmas break, Tammi and I moved back in with my grandparents. I was in fourth grade, and it was the first time that she and I went to separate schools. I had to ride a bus for the first time, which was an adventure. I knew one person, the fifth-grade neighbor girl that we played with over the summer when we visited. It was interesting to be away from Tammi from the time I went to catch the bus until she came home. I didn't feel responsible for watching over her since she wasn't with me. I was alone but didn't feel lonely.

After the court hearing was over, and the summer ended in 1978, we went back to live with my dad in Maryland. We moved into an apartment complex called Gorman Manor. Tammi and I shared a room, and we each had our canopy beds; mine was blue, and hers was pink. They were beautiful, so princess-like. We walked to school again; it was just behind the apartment building, and I had a key for us to get back in our home. We played and watched TV until my dad would get home from work. He prepared our dinner each night and then would let us fix his hair with ribbons and barrettes, just like any father would.

Daddy was still in the army at this point, and he received his new orders, transferring him to Okinawa, Japan. He knew that he couldn't take the two of us girls there alone, so he resigned his commission, and we moved back to Pennsylvania to live with my grandparents. He showed me that parents are to put what is in the best interest of their children ahead of what their desires might be.

In the summer of 1979, Tammi and I became a threesome when we met the new neighbor girl living next door to my grandparents; her name was Missy. Her mom was recently divorced, like our dad. We thought it would be wonderful if they got married so we could all be sisters. We had a great summer, and I started sixth grade at the same school I finished fourth grade; Southmoreland Elementary. Some people remembered me in my class, and it was a fun school year because all three of us were in the same building.

My dad, now working with my grandfather at C&C Lumber, and Missy's mom did start dating. In January of the following year, they married. Not only did we get Missy as a sister, but we also got an older brother and younger brother—our version of The Brady Bunch. We moved into my stepmother's house, and we three girls shared a room. We all had dinner together every evening as a family. We girls would take turns setting the table, washing, and drying the dishes each night. We did things together as a family, like weekend outings and vacations. There was no alcohol, no fighting—a calm and hopeful household. We were all settling into our new lives as a blended family.

CHAPTER 2 LIFE-CHANGING EVENT

BEING ABLE TO ASK FOR HELP IS A SIGN OF SPIRITUAL STRENGTH

Raven betrayed and abandoned;

Overwhelmed;

Takes on the responsibilities of others.

As adults, we never know when the darkness will come into our lives. As a child, it's not something that you expect or anticipate. It's not something that a child can even understand. A child still has the original connection to the Universe and talks to God and expects an answer. This connection allows the child who is overwhelmed by the darkness to have true resilience and strength in her spirit. She sees strangers helping her; she sees doors open; sees that light comes through the tiniest of places — and she learns to survive.

Between 1978 and 1980, Tammi and I only saw my mother one time. The visit occurred when she was moving across the country to Albuquerque, New Mexico. I think she was attracted to the large Native American population there. Somewhere that the people looked like her, with almond-shaped chocolate eyes and straight black hair- where mom felt she would fit it — a place where she could be her Native self.

In the summer of 1980, my mother asked my dad if Tammi and I could come out to visit her in New Mexico for the summer. She had told my dad she had been to Alcoholics Anonymous and was no longer drinking. Tammi and I missed her and wanted to go. Initially, my dad agreed but changed his mind about a week before we were to leave. He had concerns that my mother would resume drinking, as she repeatedly did while they were married. I got distraught and thought about running away—to my grandmother's house next door. I took a very long walk in the woods and calmed down enough to try to talk to my dad about allowing us to go. He consented, to my great surprise. Sometimes the Universe works to prevent anguish and pain, but God does not override our conscious decisions or our free will.

The following week, my dad took Tammi and me to the Greyhound bus station in Pittsburgh. We would travel across the country for three days to visit my mother in Albuquerque. We had books and snacks with us to keep us busy, and my dad gave me plenty of cash—more than I had ever seen—so we could eat at the rest stops. As we were preparing to leave, my dad bent down to hug Tammi goodbye, told her he loved her, and put her on the bus. He turned to me, lifted my chin, and told me, "take care of your baby sister." He kissed my forehead, and I boarded the bus, excited about the adventure.

Tammi and I sat behind the salt-and-pepper haired bus driver, who always wore a smile on his round face. We had a good time singing with the radio that he was playing. When we stopped, I bought us food, and we ate. The bus driver monitored us and made sure we were in our seats before we made our way to the next station. Each stop was the same until we got to Texas, where we had to change buses. The bus driver got our suitcases and took us to the last bus we would ride, making sure we got on the correct one. God watches over us through strangers if we are open to His love.

When we arrived at the Albuquerque bus station, Tammi and I couldn't find mom. They had to page her a few times over the intercom before she found us. As she walked towards us, her straight, raven black hair was swinging behind her as if we were lost, and she had to find us. She wore fitted jeans with a yellow T-shirt that was tight across her chest and a pair of wedge sandals, so she looked taller than her four-foot-ten inches. She had large sunglasses on, and I wondered if she was hiding bloodshot eyes. Tammi ran to her as I struggled with the suitcases before a short man wearing cowboy boots and a Stetson hat came over and took them from me.

His name was Alan; he was a nuclear physicist working at Los Alamos. He was friendly and had agreed to come with mom to pick us up since she didn't have a car. He took us out to dinner at the restaurant at the top of the Sandia Peak Tramway that ascends the Sandia Mountains. I felt out of place in this upscale atmosphere, since Tammi and I wore shorts and tank tops. We had a fancy meal with dessert before we walked around the mountain top. It was a magical place. I knew that something life-changing was going to happen, and I was happy to be here.

As Alan was dropping us off at my mother's apartment, he gave me his business card and told me that if I need anything to call him. This action surprised me since he didn't know me. I thanked him and put it in my suitcase. Maybe he was concerned because he knew the area where she lived was one of the most unsafe in the city. Or perhaps it was because he knew my mother and was concerned about her drinking while we were visiting. God always provides support; our part is to notice.

The one-bedroom studio apartment was sparse. There was a small metal dinette set off of the galley kitchen where we cooked and ate dinner each night. In the living room, a little brown couch centered in front of the TV. In the single bedroom, a full-size mattress lay on the green-carpeted floor, which we all shared. Mom made us peanut butter and jelly sandwiches for lunch each day; we went swimming every day with a friend of hers while she worked at the dry cleaners. The first two weeks of our eight-week trip were terrific. Then she started drinking. I don't know what caused her to start; I don't know if we stressed her having to care for the two of us, or if something else was going on. Still, she was an alcoholic, and my co-dependent behaviors kicked on.

While she went to work each day, Tammi and I stayed in the studio apartment and watched TV — game shows and soap operas. Mom would come home for lunch since the dry cleaner was only a block away, and I started to make the peanut butter and jelly sandwiches each day. When she came home after her shift was over, she would begin dinner and start drinking; then I would finish the cooking and serve the meal. By 10 p.m., she was passed out on the couch. So, I would cover her with a blanket, and Tammi and I would go to bed.

Although my mother was a functional alcoholic and could hold down a job, she couldn't do much more once the drinking started. I'm a reasonable observer; fortunately, I had learned her weekly habits for paying the bills. I would take her paycheck on Friday and get the check cashed at the grocery store, buy a money order for the weekly rent payment, and then buy groceries for us. Any cash I had left, I hid, in case we needed it during the week. On our way back to the apartment with the groceries that Tammi and I could carry, we would stop and give the money order to the office girl for the rent.

My mother is a mean drunk. Into week four of our visit, she began having outbursts daily, and they were directed at me. She would blame me for everything that went wrong in her life. I was the reason my dad left her, even though she left my dad. I was the reason she drank, but she drank before I was born. I was the reason she had no money, yet I was the one paying the rent each week. So, she would drink; she would blame; then, she would hit. Once she started hitting, I did the best I could to get between her and Tammi; I was doing what my dad told me to do… "take care of your baby sister." Soon, I became the one she hit regularly. Before the divorce, she would beat us with a wooden spoon, but now she was using her hand or throwing whatever she could get her hands on.

I asked Tammi about calling daddy so we could go home, but she wanted to stay. She liked the freedom we had during the day, and she thought it was fun. Besides, she and mom would cuddle on the couch while I finished making dinner, so her experience differed significantly from my own. I didn't want to upset Tammi by having us leave early, and I didn't want to get my mother in trouble with my dad because she was drinking again, as he feared. I allowed the co-dependent behavior to take over. I rationalized that it was more important to keep mom safe than it was for Tammi and me to be safe. She was more important than we were.

Soon, she started to invite her friends over, on the condition that they would bring her more alcohol. Some of these people were a little scary looking because my mother had graduated from being an alcoholic to also being a drug addict. I became the bartender again. I had an alternative system now — serve one drink, dump one drink. If I found any pills or joints, I flushed those down the toilet so my sister would not get into them. My mother allowed Tammi to take sips of her drink, and then, suddenly, Tammi had her own glass. As people would start to pass out, I would cover them with sheets and carry Tammi to bed. I began to lock the bedroom door each night, too.

One-night, Tammi passed out rather early, and I carried her to bed. As I continued to serve drinks, I saw my mother's best friend, Sally, go into the bedroom. She came out of the bedroom and then went into the bathroom. When she came out, I went into the bathroom, and, to my dismay, I found a syringe in the garbage can. I had seen the other guests use them, and I knew it made them happy before they fell asleep. I immediately ran into the bedroom to check on Tammi.

She was sound asleep, her brown wavy hair all around her head like a halo, looking peaceful. Not fully understanding what I was doing, I checked her pulse by laying my head on her small chest. She had a strong and steady heartbeat. I paid careful attention to her breathing, which was very regular, by watching the rise and fall of the kitten imprinted on her nightgown. I kept checking on her until everyone passed out, and I made sure that no one else went into the bedroom that evening. Once everyone seemed to be asleep, I covered everyone up with blankets and went to bed. In the bedroom, I locked the door behind me. I verified that there were no changes in Tammi's condition. I had a hard time falling asleep as the terror of my reality began to settle around me, but I eventually did.

I did not hear them unlock the door. I awoke to a gag in my mouth as someone was tying my hands above my head. Another person was holding my legs down. I recognized my abusers, men who had been drinking with my mother over the past few days. I didn't cry out because I didn't want Tammi to wake up, or for her to get hurt. I had to "take care of my baby sister." I was aware of what was happening, but I wasn't in my body. Tears slid down my face as I saw my mother, in the corner of the room, watching. When Sally's ex-husband was done, he and the other two men left, and Sally untied my hands. My mother and her best friend allowed three men to molest me that night.

My mother was utterly aware of what was happening and did nothing to stop it. I didn't understand why she didn't help me. I couldn't understand what I had done to justify this abuse. Sally told me a few months later that she and my mother were given drugs for their compliance. The next morning mom disappeared for a few days. I was truly alone and doing my best, at eleven years old, to "take care of my baby sister" — and to say nothing for myself.

Tammi slept for three days. I assumed they had drugged her with something, but her heartbeat and breathing were stable as I checked on her hourly. If it wasn't for the need to take care of Tammi, I'm not sure what I would have done. For the first time, I was utterly alone. I didn't know what to do. I couldn't call daddy because I was ashamed that I had failed, and we were in this chaos. When Tammi woke up, she was tired for a day, but I thought she was okay. She remembered nothing that had happened and didn't realize how long she slept. She ate and ate, then she cried and cried because I didn't know where mom was or if she was coming back.

Mom returned home on a Friday afternoon, with her paycheck, and acted as if nothing had happened. She gave me the check and told Tammi and me to go to the grocery store. I don't know why, but before we left, I got the cash I had hidden in my suitcase from the bedroom closet along with Alan's business card. We cashed the check, purchased the money order for the rent, and bought groceries. As we walked back to the apartment, I saw my mother waiting for us on the front stoop. She took the grocery bags from us and went inside while Tammi and I went to pay the rent. When we came back, she had our suitcases out on the front stoop and sternly told us it was time for us to go home. She went inside and locked the door behind her.

Tammi started screaming and crying. She pounded her little fists on the door, begging mom to let us in. The tape playing in my head for the past two weeks about taking care of my baby sister played again. I calmed Tammi down and said we needed to call daddy so we could go home. She didn't argue with me this time. I was planning on going to the police station to make the call, but she wanted to go to my mother's best friend's house. I consented to keep her calm, and, this way, I wouldn't get mom into trouble. My co-dependent nature to protect mom was still in effect, despite the harrowing conditions.

Looking back at this memory, I realize this is the moment that
the independent and fearless little girl that my grandmother
described utterly took over. The fear welling up, the heartache I
was experiencing, the desperation I was feeling ended. I knew
that I needed to take charge of the situation for Tammi and me to
return home safely. I knew that I could do it. I just needed some
Divine intervention.

We walked the streets of Albuquerque with our suitcases to
Sally's home, which was over a mile away. No-one stopped us
to ask if we were okay as they were too busy sleeping next to the
buildings or looking for food in the trash cans. Seeing two little
girls walking the thoroughfares as they struggled to carry the
two suitcases didn't cause any alarms in this troubling area of
town. When we arrived at Sally's place, Tammi ran into her
arms, crying and telling her mom kicked us out. As she consoled
Tammi, I asked if I could use the phone to call my dad; she
nodded.

I only remember bits and pieces of the conversation with my
dad. I didn't cry. In a calm voice, I told him that mom was
ready for us to come home, we were not allowed back into her
apartment, and that we needed to leave now. I don't recall if I
told him she was drinking. He made a comment about calling
the police, but since I didn't want my mother to get into trouble,
I told him we didn't need the police. He asked if we were in a
safe place, and I remember saying we were — but only for a little
while. I remember that he had to call us back once he had
arrangements made, and when daddy did, he told me we had
airplane tickets waiting for us at the airport for the following
day.

I didn't want to spend the night at Sally's house. But Tammi felt
safe and didn't want us to leave, so I agreed to spend the night
there — it wasn't as if we had anywhere else to stay. My dad

asked if we had a way to the airport, and I said I had someone I could call, and if that didn't work out, I had enough money for a taxicab. He didn't ask me where I got the money. He said he would meet us when the plane landed the next night and that I was to take care of my baby sister.

I called Alan, the nuclear physicist who had come with my mom to pick us up from the bus station. When he answered the phone, and I told him what happened, he said he would be happy to take us to the airport the next morning. He didn't ask any questions except the address, and Sally gave it to him. When the Divine brings an end to a situation, He continually releases hidden blessings to help guide us through to safety.

All we had to do was get through the next sixteen hours with the person who suggested to my mother that she could get more drugs by instigating my molestation and the person who drugged Tammi. My sister, unaware, fell asleep quickly on the couch, exhausted from the day's traumas. I did not sleep while we were there. I sat at the kitchen table all night watching the clock, watching over my baby sister. Throughout the night, the terror tried to escape my body as I trembled, but the fear only grew as the clock slowly ticked the minutes away.

At some point early the next morning, Sally came and sat down at the table with me.

As she sipped her coffee, she said, "I know you want to protect your sister, right?"

I nodded my head in affirmation.

She leered at me with her dark eyes and said, "You aren't going to tell anyone what your mother did to you, right? Because the same could happen to Tammi if you do."

I just stared at her while my heart was pounding in my chest, fear welling up from deep within me.

"I have friends everywhere, and we'll be watching you. So, if you do tell anyone, I will know."

She stared at me with an eerie gaze in silence for what seemed like an hour before she got up from the table.

My hands were shaking, and I believed every word she told me. The horror of what my life became appeared in full focus, and I shuddered. Fear is a tremendous force that can completely change how you view the world and everyone in it.

Alan arrived right on time, and he took Tammi and me to the airport where the tickets were waiting for us at the counter. We thanked Alan, and he saw that we safely boarded the airplane. We had to change aircraft in Denver, and our flight was a little delayed, so we had to run with the stewardess through the terminal to make the connecting flight. Once on board the second plane, I finally slept, like a rock, after being awake for over twenty-four hours. I slept through a meal and a snack service. It took hearing Tammi calling my name to awaken me as we were pulling up to the terminal at the Pittsburgh airport.

When we landed, my dad, in his blue button-down shirt and khaki pants, was waiting for us at the end of the jetway. Tammi ran to him and jumped into his arms, smiling and telling him about the flight. I approached apprehensively, thinking he must be able to see the damage that had befallen me because I convinced him to let us visit mom. As I hugged him, daddy looked down at me, and I told him that Tammi and I needed therapy as soon as possible. My stepmother had been in treatment, and I knew it was a safe place that could help. He nodded his head, acknowledging what I had said, and asked if I was okay. I said I was, and I just wanted to go home. I was aware; I knew what happened was wrong, but wasn't sure what to do. I knew we needed help. I didn't know what kind of help I needed, but I asked. Being able to ask for help is the surest sign of spiritual strength.

CHAPTER 3 PEOPLE ALONG THE PATH

SURVIVORSHIP IS A CHOICE TO HEAL

Raven lost and full of fear;

Protection removed-

Feeling alone,

In the darkness.

Since I didn't understand what happened to me, I started to ask questions. The main question I asked was, "why?" Why did this happen? Why didn't God help me? Why did my dad allow me to go? Why doesn't my mother love me? Why did she abandon us? The reality is that I may never know the answer to the "why," because I cannot honestly understand the reasons these people did what they did. I cannot understand my mother's suffering. I cannot know her pain. I cannot understand her motives for her bad behavior.

When I couldn't figure out the answers to the "why" questions, I started to blame, and I first blamed myself. What did I do to deserve this? How could I have stopped this from happening? What did I do so God wouldn't help me? How could my dad be convinced that we should visit my mother? Blame is a tool of the ego. When it is turned inward, it is called guilt. It can be used as a self-defense mechanism but blame takes us on a painful journey that we consciously choose to go on.

On Monday, after we arrived back home in Pennsylvania, my dad took Tammi and me to see a counselor. We went a couple of times a week for a few weeks of evaluation. At the end of the evaluation period, Tammi was deemed okay and didn't need to see a therapist anymore; I, however, needed more therapy, and they suggested a psychiatrist. The first thing the doctor tried to do was to medicate me. Thankfully, my dad didn't agree with medications. I wasn't clinically depressed, I wasn't anxious, but everyone knew something wasn't right.

No medication meant that I didn't need to see the psychiatrist. So, I started to see a psychotherapist, and her name was Denise. She was a nice lady with a bob of dark hair and soft, caring eyes. She did want to help me but never asked me any of the hard questions. We talked about the new, blended family I was a part of, about Tammi, about the school I was attending, about everything except my mother. Although I knew I needed to go to counseling, I wasn't sure what to do when I got there. Talking about things that upset me, especially my mother, was something I felt should be avoided because it was painful. So, when she asked what I wanted to talk about, I would choose anything other than the trip to New Mexico. I only went to therapy for five years. During this time, we only talked about the abandonment a few times, and at no time did we discuss the sexual abuse.

I spent the rest of the summer, after returning from New Mexico, at home, mostly sleeping or walking in the woods. Becoming very talkative with God, I asked Him many questions. Why was the only time I felt safe now when I was alone in the woods? Why was I scared all the time when I was with other people, even my family? What did I do to anger Him? But I didn't feel that I received any answers — or, at least, answers that I could understand. I was spending too much time in my head trying to figure out what happened, what went wrong, how I could have prevented it all from happening. At eleven years old, turning inward, allowing the ego to wall-off my authenticity, closed me off from God and others. The ego is the part of ourselves whose job it is to protect us from harm, real or imagined. It was trying to protect me from being hurt and abandoned again. Still, in the process, I shut down my emotions completely.

Everyone at home was careful when they spoke to me, and purposely left me alone. I liked being left alone. I didn't feel guilty about staying away from them. I was losing my connection with my family. This loss caused my egoic mind to form the terrifying belief that they, too, would abandon me. During this time, I don't remember getting upset or crying; I was just there. I lay on my bed, listening to the radio. I would join everyone for the family dinner. I would do whatever chores I was to do. I was numb, no highs, no lows. Even when I went for a hike in the woods, I wasn't present. I was locked in my head, building the wall around me to close myself off from everyone. I was doing what my ego thought would keep me safe.

School starting back up in the fall of 1980 forced me to be with other people and, therefore, required more of me than just existing. As I entered the seventh grade, the start of junior high, there was apprehension. I am sure that the transition is daunting for everyone. Still, once I had schoolwork to do, I had a purpose. I had something I could focus my mind on instead of wallowing in guilt. What happened to me in Albuquerque was my fault because I failed to take care of my baby sister. I was blaming myself for my mother abandoning us. I was guilty of wanting to be alone and of the sin of wanting to die, so my suffering would end.

I was taking all advanced classes, which required me to do much studying. I tried to get out of the elective courses by taking more science and history but wasn't allowed, so I was in the school chorus. Chorus was a place of joy, and it stirred hope within me that I thought had died. Singing, for me, was a way to connect to the creative part of myself. It reminded me of my dad giving me a brush to use as a microphone and standing me on top of the coffee table so I could sing at the top of my little lungs Debby Boone's "You Light Up My Life." Choir forced me to sing again. I felt the fluttering of my heart when I was chosen to participate in a small ensemble group of talented singers called the Scottiettes. I loved singing songs full of happy emotions, the feelings I separated myself from the past few months. Hopefulness is the faith one has when there is no visible sign that everything will turn out well.

This school year was the time I learned to play the pretending game. My family, my teachers, my friends all wanted me to be okay. So, to keep them believing that I was fine, I pretended I was okay. I acted the part. By doing so, I didn't have to deal with any negative feelings or memories of the past. Then, one Saturday night, I accidentally spoke to my mother.

My mother had been calling Tammi every couple of weeks after we returned, but I wouldn't talk to her. Tammi knew that I didn't want to talk to her. When she would ask me, I would get overtly hostile, which was not my nature, especially with my sister. That evening Tammi called for me to come up to our room, saying I had a phone call but not telling me who was calling. I went up to take the call as she left the room. I said, "Hello."

I heard my mother's smokey voice, "Hello, baby, how are you?"

"Fine, thank you. I hope you're doing well," I politely responded as I heard in my head, *Honor thy mother and thy father*.

"Well, I'm not," she spewed, as she started to raise her voice, "and it is all your fault!"

Fear started to swell inside my chest as I knew that she had been drinking. I began to cry silently. There was an internal conflict of honoring my mother while at the same time wanting to protect myself rose within me.

"Why did you have to be born?" she slurred. "If you didn't, I would still be with your father. I'd be sober. I'd still have Tammi; she's just like me. Terri, it's all your fault, you ruined my life. I hate you!"

I hurled the phone across the room, and as I watched it smash into pieces against the wall I started to shriek, "It's not my fault, it's not my fault.... it's not my fault!" I crumbled to the floor sobbing.

The next thing I remember is my dad trying to get ahold of me. He's trying to hug me as I'm trying to pull away, still screaming, but he holds on to me. I'm crying into his chest, and he's rocking me back and forth...back and forth...back and forth. Once I'm exhausted, just whimpering, he tries to lay me down, but I wake up and start crying again. All night long, I was in his arms. My dad was a beautiful example of how our heavenly Father cares and comforts His children.

This mental breakdown caused my mother to stop calling. My dad told her not to call anymore until she had gotten her drinking under control. Not being able to speak to my mother, of course, upset Tammi, who also got in trouble for tricking me so that I would take the phone call in the first place. She had no idea what happened to me the night she was drugged. Tammi didn't understand my fearful response to my mother's lies. She was a victim, too, a victim of mom's manipulation to get what she wanted—to blame me for her choices.

Being the oldest girl in the family, I was riding the bus to the school by myself. This bus was for junior and senior high school students. I would sit in the front of the bus because I was the last to be picked up, and the bus was full, but the bus driver would make the people in the front seat move over to make room for me. When the white winter snows arrived, my grandmother bought me a rabbit fur coat, and it was so soft. There was a high school senior named Dino who would pet the jacket as he got off the bus each afternoon. After a while, he would holler for me when I got on the bus in the morning that he saved me a seat in the back. He didn't do much talking to me, but he kept petting the coat. He also wouldn't let anyone else touch the jacket or tease me. I soon thought of him as my protector.

About this time, since I was in the bus's back seat, I noticed a navy-blue minivan that seemed to be following the bus. Each morning when I got on the bus, the van was behind us. It would follow us the whole way to the school campus. After a few weeks, my egoic mind started to make me believe what Sally told me; that she had friends everywhere, and they were watching me then reporting back to her. It didn't help that she also started to call regularly to check on Tammi and me since my mother could no longer call. As she repeated her threat of hurting Tammi, she would remind me that she had people watching me.

A few years later, in high school, one of the teacher's aide mentioned seeing me wait for the bus each morning. She had started her position on campus when I first noticed the minivan following the bus. I realized that it was her, not someone that Sally sent to watch me. When the ego is allowed to go unchecked as you respond to the world around you from a place of fear, the mere coincidences of life can be seen as threats.

Once summer vacation arrived and I had no homework, my mind turned back to the negative thoughts. Blaming and guilt again took over. Destructive pictures of everyone leaving me would run through my mind. Scenarios played out of how much danger I was in when I was with other people, and fear would settle into the very core of my being. The dread of others. The panic at being in enclosed places. The terror of being abandoned. The anxiety of being touched. Fear became my state of being. It was all-encompassing. I felt utterly alone, which is what fear does; it isolates us.

My grandparents had moved back to their hometown of Mt.

Pleasant, and my grandfather was working part-time on Saturdays at C&C Lumber. After work, he would come by and pick me up so I could spend time with them. We would have dinner together and then walk to St. Pius X Roman Catholic church for mass. Then I would spend the night with them and go home the next afternoon.

Going to church was the start of my search for answers. It was the start of figuring out what I was supposed to do with what had happened to me — the abandonment and sexual abuse. I would pray, read the Bible that my grandmother had previously gotten for me, and attend any church service that I could. That connection I felt to God had not gone away; I didn't seem to understand how I felt about Him or the other people around me, so I kept probing.

Part of not understanding how I felt was due to me shutting down my emotions. After the breakdown on the phone with my mother, my dad was more concerned and more watchful, which is understandable. I again went back to playing the game and wearing the mask, being what they wanted me to be so that they wouldn't worry. Yet I wanted to be left alone. Being in emotional distress is not the time to be alone; suffering allows the ego to take over the mind. Defense mechanisms had taken hold of my mind. I practiced avoidance, masked as good study habits, and staying busy. My control issues were disguised as being organized and able to lead others. Logical thinking was camouflaged by getting good grades so I could hide my emotions. These defense mechanisms have their place and were very helpful for some time. The ego uses them to help us survive, but they become harmful when we do not let go of them and do not grow into the person we are meant to be.

As I moved through the next few years into high school from 1982 through 1985, I continued to keep to myself and spent as much time in any church that I could. I was questioning the meaning and value of my life, since I now felt abandoned by God, too. I had a group of a few friends that I did things with through the eleventh grade. Susie was my best friend, and I give her full credit in helping me to have a semi-normal teenage experience. She was a beautiful blonde-haired, blue-eyed pageant participant who could tap dance and sing. I met her as part of the Scottiettes. Born and raised in the community, she knew everyone. I adored her parents, who were loving and allowed me to be in their home as much as I wanted. Susie was an only child, and we bonded during our freshman year of high school. Because of her, I dressed up for Halloween, went to school dances, football, and basketball games, and made a few other friends. Susie helped me to realize that I was intelligent. She encouraged me when it came to boys and helped me with developing my colorful sense of style.

Complications arose with the onset of dating. Being touched was something I avoided, so being alone with a boy could put me in a situation that brought back memories of the rape. The concept of dating and spending time with a boy did not seem to bother me, but doing it alone was very uncomfortable. I would go out with a group of friends which I enjoyed. In my sophomore year, I did have a boyfriend, Carl. He was definitely what my parents thought of as a bad-boy type. He appeared to be a tough guy who liked hard rock music, had shoulder-length, jet black hair, went to vo-tech, and smoked. Despite all of this, what really bothered my parents was that he briefly dated both Tammi and my stepsister Missy before dating me.

Carl was around the house quite often with Tammi and Missy, so I started getting used to him, and over time my defenses came down. He would see me in the hallway at school and would say hi. I was timid and withdrawn at school, and as Carl got to see more of the real me, he was surprised that I wasn't that way at home. We would talk about school, and he would ask me questions; more importantly, he listened to what I had to say.

Listening was significant to me. I was talking to others, hinting at things, but people didn't seem to be listening. Carl was the first person I opened up to about what happened with my mother in New Mexico. He was cautious with me. He allowed me to go on and on about the anger, rage, heartbreak, isolation, and endless fear.

Betsy, Carl's mother, went to a Methodist church each Sunday morning. I asked her if she would take me, and she agreed. She was delighted to do this because it meant that Carl would go too. So Saturday night, I went to the Roman Catholic Church with my grandparents. Then Sunday mornings, I went to Sunday school and a Methodist service. I was searching for understanding, for answers, for closure, for peace.

Carl was a very caring individual behind the bravado. He was both emotionally and physically abused by his stepfather. Therefore, Carl could relate on an emotional level to some of what I was going through. Very understanding of my wounds, he was gentle with me. We went to school dances together as well as other group functions: football games, basketball games, wrestling matches, drama productions. For two years, we dated, even though we were rarely alone.

In the summer of 1985, between my junior and senior years of high school, we moved to a bigger house in a different town. I was to start at a new school for my senior year. This decision upset Susie so much that her parents spoke to my dad about me living with them my senior year so I could graduate with my class. I was surprised by the offer and even more surprised that my dad discussed it with me.

I did think about staying with Susie and Carl, but I chose not to leave my family. The decision upset Carl. It was sweet that he wanted me to stay with him. I rationalized that the move would be good for me—a new house, a room of my own, people who didn't know me—a fresh start. Unable to understand what I needed to do; he broke up with me that summer before my senior year of high school. Although it hurt me that we parted ways, I remember realizing that Carl made me comprehend that guys could be safe to be around. That my past experiences in New Mexico were not the only ones that could happen — there were more possibilities of loving-kindness if I would open up to the prospects.

My senior year in a new high school was daunting. It was almost ten times as big as the school I had moved from, so the number of teenagers in the building was staggering. I went from a graduating class of about 225 to a class size of 1,975 people. I was an unnoticed speck with no background, no friends, no history — I was in paradise. As I started classes, a girl named Elise befriended me. She was tall, with short blonde hair and bright blue eyes, and she carried a Bible. The Bible is what drew me to her. I asked her all kinds of questions about her faith, and she invited me to go to a youth group with her. She said it would be a group of teenagers from her boyfriend's church; we would play volleyball, have some snacks, and talk a little. I was intrigued and agreed to attend since it was only about a half-mile from our new home, and she could pick me up on the way.

As we entered the community building, I saw the volleyball net was up, and a few people were tossing the ball. Elise went to her boyfriend and brought him over to meet me. Tall with brown hair and caring green eyes, he was much older than I thought he would be. He was friendly and introduced me to the group. We played a few games of volleyball, ate some snacks, and then had a devotional time. During this time, I recognized one of the guys that rode the school bus with me. He seemed to have a girlfriend with him but kept looking at me. After the devotional Elise introduced me to him, Scott was his name. She said a few of them were going out for pizza and asked if I wanted to come with them before they took me home, and I said sure.

Scott ended up meeting us at the pizza place. He pulled up a chair next to me and started talking to Elise's boyfriend. Every so often, Scott would ask me a question. I asked where his girlfriend was, and he said he broke up with her before he met up with us. He gave me a big smile. I was surprised by this behavior, and it made me uncomfortable. What would cause him to change how he felt about someone so suddenly?

Scott and I ended up dating the end of our senior year of high school. I wanted a prom date, so it all worked out. We went to Sunday school and church together at the Assemblies of God church that his parents and grandparents attended. The youth group was on Friday evenings until we graduated. Scott had bushy blond hair, blue eyes, and was a bit shy, and I liked that. He was smart and exceptionally mechanically inclined — if it was broke, he could fix it. A lot of his time was spent rebuilding a dirt bike, working on his Beetle, and working at the local gas station.

I fell in love with his family, especially his mother, Linda. Not a typical redhead, she was timid and reserved. She was a very loving, tenderhearted person. She was an attentive and caring mother. Linda was close to her parents and had always lived near the house where she was raised, so she never really got out on her own. She would say that she had low self-esteem, which she did. She had a thyroid issue after her second son was born, which caused her to gain weight, which made her self-esteem issues more prominent.

She was able to see my pain very quickly, as it paralleled her own. Through this pain, we bonded. I was comfortable with her and could easily share my thoughts, my pain, and my past with her and felt no judgment. She was the first adult that I was not playing the game with — the game of pretending that I was all right, and it was okay. There were no negative repercussions for me being the ugly, negative me that I was at the time.

My time with Linda allowed me to see that my brokenness wasn't a part of who I was supposed to be; it wasn't my authentic self. Whether I see myself as a victim or a survivor, this self-image has a direct bearing on how my life will progress.

As a victim, I became self-focused, I'd go inward and allow the suffering to grow. I blamed others, my mother and Sally, for how I felt and believed people were trying to hurt me intentionally. A victim, even years later, is still powerless. Victimhood has dire consequences that I had to outgrow.

I survived the incredible hurt and betrayal, yes, but that survival didn't make me a survivor. A survivor embraces life and doesn't hide from it due to fear. I wore my victimhood for about ten years. Mainly because I was only eleven when the abuse occurred, and I didn't know how to deal with the feelings of anger, despair, and horrendous fear.

Despite being in therapy through high school, I wasn't able to let go of playing the victim as I continued to live in the past. As a victim, I had little responsibilities other than school. People felt sorry for me and were very careful not to upset me. Being left alone was what I thought I wanted.

During the next three years of college, I started to see that other people weren't necessarily all bad. Maybe it was because we were all in a new situation, and making friends helped us cope with the newfound independence we all had. I realized that I was creating some of the drama that was around me as I was observing others around me doing the same thing. Then, I had someone tell me that I liked my victimhood more than I wanted to be a survivor!

Wow — how dare he say that to me? He had no idea what I had survived. After my initial bout of anger rose out of me, I listened to what he had to say. To become a survivor, I had to give up the idea that I was a victim and learn from the experience.

For me to be an overcomer, I had to learn a new language that is devoid of blame. It meant that, as a survivor, I had to take responsibility for the choices I had made since the abuse. The decisions I made were ultimately the cause of the situation I was now in—not the mistreatment.

Yes, I was abused. Yes, it caused me to think negatively, but the choices I had made since the abuse were my responsibility, no one else's. I decided not to talk to the therapist about the sexual abuse. I chose not to use the professional help I asked for when we returned. By letting go of the blame, I also let go of the helplessness. I couldn't feel like a victim and live like a survivor. Blaming others meant that they're the ones in control of my life, not me; therefore, I chose to be a survivor and take back control of my life. Victims feel helpless, whereas survivors have reclaimed their power and taken back control of their lives. Through survivorship, I took responsibility for my choices and my feelings and consciously decided that I'm no longer a victim. Survivorship is a choice to heal. And I simply made a decision that I was going to survive and not be a victim.

I realized all my suffering began with beliefs I had that went unchallenged. The longer I allowed these thoughts to affect my life and emotions, the more I suffered. I am the observer of the ideas. I don't need to believe that they are right; most often, they aren't. To examine my thoughts, I needed to look at them from a logical perspective versus an emotional one.

Reframing the story of my victimization does not mean lying about it or forgetting what happened. It's about looking at it from the lessons I learned about myself as a survivor. For example, I am a survivor of child sexual abuse and abandonment—why is that important? Yes, the experience was awful, but I know now that I have enough strength and compassion to help others overcome the fear in their lives. That's my mission; despite being victimized, I made a conscious decision to be a survivor.

When I was going through the traumatic event, and for a long time afterward, it was hard to look at things from a different perspective. As time passed, I gained alternative viewpoints. It's through this reframing of my story that I did while in college, I created the change I desired in my life.

The stories I told myself created my life. The versions established my identities and the kind of person that I thought I was. The stories also gave my life meaning, helped me to make sense of the world, and guided my actions, even from a young age. Built into my nature is the ability to gain perspective over time if I'm willing to alter my mindset.

I needed to start paying attention to the stories that I told myself and others. The key is to remember that I'm the storyteller; therefore, I can view my account in any way I deem. That is, I can reframe my story so that it serves and supports me instead of harming my life.

After all, it's not the impartial world that affects me, but how I characterize and understand the world. In other words, what matters isn't what happened to me, but the stories I tell myself about what took place. I formed my reality based on signals which bring to mind my beliefs about the world and myself. As a result, I either end up feeling good or feeling bad.

The first thing I needed to do was to learn not to react in the way I'd done in the past, which was to keep feeling bad. Feelings are something I can choose to sense. So, instead of feeling bad, I could pick a better mood. To make this switch, the second thing that I needed to ensure was that I had to change the meaning of what occurred. As I altered the connotation of the event, I could revise the feelings I associated with the occasion.

Reframing is a way of viewing events, ideas, concepts, and

emotions to find more useful alternatives. It's a practical and valuable tool to shift perception. Think of reframing as putting on a different pair of glasses. What would I see if I put on a pair of sunglasses in a dark room? I would see shadows and dark forms I couldn't identify. However, when I take off the glasses, I see something beautiful. And when I switch my lenses, what I see changes. Reframing altered the story I told myself about what happened.

When I was told by a college friend that I was getting something for playing the victim of abuse instead of living as a survivor, I became aware. I had an "aha moment." I awakened from the stupor of pain to realize that, a decade after the abuse, I was causing my continued suffering. Only when I became aware could I change my mindset and, therefore, my life.

I was choosing to relive my story of abuse and abandonment by my mother each day. Looking back on this, it seems irrational to relive a terrible experience over and over again. But I did it, and it wasn't helping me in any way. I was ashamed for allowing this event to have such a negative power over me for so long. However, I was not to shift the blame from the abuser to myself. I needed to take responsibility for my actions. By taking responsibility, I reclaimed my power over the story, and only then could I reframe it.

Through what other perspectives could I view the trauma I lived through when I was a child? As a teenager, I was unable to see any other version of my story. But due to my college friend, I saw a different perception of those events. I could see myself as a survivor of child sexual abuse. Survivorship is a positive way to view trauma because I did survive the ordeal.

So, I took back my power and became a survivor, not a victim. I reframed my story. I chose to change my victimization story to one of survivorship. This step was vital to creating a new vision for my life. This reframing wasn't an overnight process. It took about three years for my ego to let go of this fearful storyline that it had perpetuated to keep me in a constant state of fear. As a result, I had days where I'd fall back into the old pattern of victimization.

Nonetheless, I now know that I can decide to re-choose how I want to live, no more victimhood, or any other negativity from the past. I can, each moment, choose to reframe the negativity into a story that is beneficial for my life.

As the author of my narrative, the way I reframe my story affects more than just me. The more responsibilities I have, and the more personal connections with others I have, the more I influence others. My story impacts my family, my friends, and even my co-workers, whether I realize it or not. This effect is because it affects me, then it affects those around me, even if they don't know my story.

My beliefs and attitudes are not hidden away, especially during times of tension. As stress increases, if I'm not fully present and aware, my ego tries to take over and pulls me back into a state of fear and old patterns. This pattern is when my past can come out for others to be affected. I first realized this when Scott was trying to get my attention, came up behind me and tapped me on the shoulder. Terror rose inside me, I made a fist, and I turned around, ready to punch him. My fear wasn't based on the current situation, but my past fears of being touched unexpectedly.

I want my story to inspire others positively. By reframing my narrative into one that moves others, I empower myself to assist others in overcoming their negative patterns. I can also help them reframe their negative comments as an illustration of how much power words have on our lives.

What lessons have I learned from my victimization? How have I become stronger? What ways have I overcome the circumstances in which I found myself? These types of questions helped me determine how I could reframe the story I told into a one of survival instead of victimhood.

From the time of the abuse until I was about nineteen years old, I lived in relentless fear. I was anxious about everything and everybody. Anxiety is one of the ways fear disguises itself. It's fear of the future. My apprehension was so bad that I was having panic attacks and would hold my breath until I passed out, as a way to deal with the fear. This defense mechanism wasn't productive and made me feel helpless and out of control.

Being fearful of the past or the future means we're not living in the present moment. Being fully present means that there's no place for depression, fear of the past, or anxiety because, in the present, I am safe.

Right now, this exact minute, I am entirely safe. A tiger is not attacking; I am writing this book. The past doesn't have any bearing on this moment unless victimhood allows it. The future has nothing to do with the present moment unless I let my thoughts go into the unknown. I can control what I think; therefore, there is no reason to fear either the past or the future. As a survivor, I make a conscious effort to live in the present moment.

When I played the victim, I tended to be solely focused on myself. Why did this happen to me? Who is going to hurt me next? Spending countless hours inside my head, reviewing the past, or playing out future scenarios are other ways I was focused inward.

As a survivor, I made a change to focus outwardly on others. This switch was difficult for me because I didn't trust others. But the survivor in me overcame the mistrust and fear because real survival comes from making connections with others.

Choose to be a survivor. Yes, it can be hard to make the change. Staying in victimhood is a pain that I was a comfortable feeling. Stepping out of my comfort zone and trying on survivorship was new and intimidating. Still, the reward of being in control of my life was incredible.

CHAPTER 4 REMOVING THE THORNY BLANKET

SETTING BOUNDARIES IS SELF-CARE

Raven covered by a thorny blanket;

Knows removal will cause pain;

The pain from healing wounds.

Help is needed but fearful of following her heart

And not her intellect.

Scott and I were engaged and supposed to get married in the fall of 1989, but he called off the engagement to date someone else. When a few months later, he heard from his mother that I was dating as well; he rekindled the engagement. For three years, I was so drawn into Scott's family that I married him despite his behavior. Looking back, I see the hand of God trying to intervene, but I so wanted Linda as my mother. I didn't listen to my intuition that marrying him was not something I should do. We married in June 1990. My countenance that day wasn't of a lucky girl marrying the love of her life, but one of resolve. I was settling for less in one area of my life so I could have something I desperately desire in another. I got Linda, and it thrilled me. I was now a part of this close-knit family. They came together every holiday, every birthday for all the nieces and nephews— any reason to celebrate and come together, they did. Now, I was a part of it, and Linda was my mother.

Due to the time I spent in church, I believed I needed to honor my mother and my father. So, I invited my mom to the wedding. I thought if we did ever reconcile, I'd be sad that she hadn't been there. Surprisingly, she came. My sister, Tammi, really stepped up and looked after her while she was in Pennsylvania. Her co-workers saved up money to buy her a native American print dress for the event. She looked much older than I thought she would. Her hair was still black, but now it was shorter with curls. Her face is where I felt she aged the most, with creases around her eyes and mouth. I danced with her, and she was kind to me. I hoped that this could be a fresh start for us. All children hope mommy will love them, and that day I had an inkling of hope.

Scott and I moved to Georgia, where he had a good job, and within a year, we had purchased a house and had our only child, Joshua. The baby was a surprise, as I was on the pill. We decided that I would stay at home and raise him, which I loved.

During the pregnancy, I was busy trying to deal with my co-dependent nature. I knew from therapy that most people who have to deal with an alcoholic become co-dependent. For me, co-dependence was cleaning up after my mom, so daddy doesn't find out. It was playing hostess to monitor how much mom is drinking. It was the way I protected my sister when mom got mad. Co-dependent behavior is something that is learned as a coping mechanism, but the practice can be passed on to our children, which does them harm. During the months I was pregnant, I worked on identifying the co-dependent behaviors I had and how to overcome them.

These co-dependent behaviors manifested not just with my mother, but with my new husband as well. I made excuses for Scott's adverse reactions, which included outbursts of anger, especially to his mother, Linda. I cleaned up the messes he made when he got angry and broke things. I learned how to navigate his mood swings. He would have a few months of a depressive state that made it hard to get him up in the morning to go to work. When he came home, he would go straight to sleep.

Then, without warning, he went into a manic state. Here he would work all day and then spend all night in the garage before going to work with little or no sleep. I read, journaled, and prayed. I also cried as I worked through these co-dependent behaviors. I must have needed over nine months to do this work because Joshua didn't arrive on his due date—he was over three weeks late; I needed the ten months to do this work.

The birth of my son was a natural one. I had no drugs and had a midwife deliver him in a hospital. Induction occurred at 7 a.m. on August 7, 1991, and he was born at 1 p.m. There was meconium in my water. Hence, the neonatal unit was in the delivery room. I wasn't concerned and believed I was finally ready for his arrival. The nurses placed him on my belly for me to see and then whisked him away so neonatal could evaluate him. Then I had some issues delivering the placenta. Complications arose, they called the doctor in and, about four hours after Joshua was born, the placenta finally released.

Two weeks before the birth of my son, I watched the movie *Switched at Birth*—very scary when you are pregnant. So, I had Scott go with the baby. I also read all the baby books, including Dr. Spock's, so I believed that there was a crucial bonding period after the baby is born, and I missed it. I felt a massive disconnect from my son. The bonding that I had read about, I did not feel. It devastated me. Fear swelled inside me because I did not want to pass on to my son the negativity I had with my mother. Luckily Joshua felt no disconnection from me.

Once Joshua was born, I often hoped that my mother would get sober so she could meet him. Tammi was taking a trip out to visit mom in New Mexico with her ten-month daughter, Stephanie, and stopped to visit us on the way. She said mom wasn't drinking, and she wanted her to meet her granddaughter while she was sober. At the last minute, I decided to go with her as I wasn't too fond of the idea of her and Stephanie driving across the country alone. The only condition I had for Tammi was that she couldn't tell mom I was coming. It had to be a surprise, as I didn't want her to start drinking before we arrived.

So off we went on our wild adventure. Twenty-two hours non-stop with two babies under the age of two—crazy! When we arrived, it stunned mom. She was so excited to meet both her grandchildren. I told her we would visit as long as she wasn't drinking, and she agreed. The next day we had a lovely time in Old Town Albuquerque with her and the two toddlers visiting the sites and enjoying one another's company. That evening she started drinking, so Joshua and I left. That August day in 1993 was the only time she ever spent with her grandson. I was happy she got to meet him but disappointed that she could only handle a day with us. The hope of reconciliation squelched again.

Three years later, in January 1996, I saw my mother for the last time. She'd been calling me a couple of times a year, and I was honoring my mother as long as she was sober. She was going back to Alaska for the first time since her adoption. Mom was taking her nephew, who was given up for adoption when he was born. Tom wanted to meet his birth mother's family, and mom agreed to introduce him. He also reached out to me, and I met them in Fairbanks for the three-day visit.

Seeing her was odd, especially since she was sober for the entire trip. She was with her recent husband, David. We spent the first evening reuniting with mom's older brother Harry and his family. It was the first time they had seen each other in over forty years. The next day we flew on a tiny airplane to Fort Yukon, eight miles inside the arctic circle. Mom was very emotional this day seeing her old house, the Episcopal church, which had a beaded altar cloth on it that her mother helped to create. We went to the cemetery where her family rested. For fun, we rode on a dog sled during the dusky three hours of light we had. It was a balmy fifty below zero without the windchill. Our final evening in Fairbanks, a potlach, or ceremonial feast, was given in our honor. I was happy to share this experience with her, and again the hope of reunification sparked but was never realized. I am glad that the last time I saw her she was sober. And that I have pictures of this remarkable time with her.

Later that year, I realized that God needed to intervene in my marriage. I had been slowing, removing myself from situations that would engage a co-dependent reaction from me. I was more than willing to stay married to Scott for the rest of my life, as I made the conscious decision to marry him, and I knew why I did—to have Linda as my mother. But things had to change. I couldn't deal with his sudden outbursts of anger.

The event that spurred me to take action was when he punched a hole in the wall. I don't even remember what caused him to get angry, but in his rage, he made three holes in the drywall in front of our five-year-old son. Scott knew his explosion was wrong because he repaired the wall in less than twenty-four hours and never mentioned it again. This incident caused me to realize that I couldn't fix his temper, so I prayed.

Heavenly Father, I know that I married Scott for the wrong reason. I care for him, but I love his mother. I take full responsibility for my wrong choice. Forgive me for causing these circumstances; I now find myself in. Holy Spirit, show me how to repair this marriage, as I am willing to do the work necessary to make us all happy. If fixing it isn't an option, then I ask to be released from it in a way that is peaceful for all of us. Amen.

A few weeks later, on Thanksgiving, 1996, Scott told me he wanted a divorce. Eleven days later, we had signed separation papers.

I was very conscious during the divorce process and aware that I had a son with Scott, and we would have to deal with one another for at least twenty years. Scott got the house; I got custody of Joshua. I took the furniture I brought into the marriage, the new computer we purchased, the car I'd been driving, and a few thousand cash from the savings account. I left him everything else. I only asked for minimum state-mandated child support and, despite not working for the past five years, I didn't ask for spousal support. I wanted us to be able to communicate about our son without additional emotional baggage from a nasty divorce.

Joshua was a child from a split home whose parents could and would talk to one another. He couldn't tell me that dad said he could do whatever because I would pick up the phone and call his dad. Although Joshua didn't like that his dad and I got along, it was a much better environment for him. He didn't hear his parents fighting, as I did after my parent's divorce. When parents fight, especially divorced parents, it can cause significant harm to the child. Each parent is part of the child. So, when one parent spews venom about the other, the child internalizes those words as part of who he is. Children are smart. Children are intuitive. Scott and I were kind to one another for the sake of our child.

People come into your life for a reason, and they leave your life for a reason. Sometimes I try to hold on instead of letting go. This holding on keeps those who are meant to be in your life from entering. Scott had a co-worker named Phillip. Phillip was a friendly guy who was a brilliant storyteller. They were talking about women, and Phillip mentioned that he likes short, petite, dark-haired girls. Phillip would later tell me Scott said he would never introduce him to me. I am five-foot-two, weighing about one hundred pounds with dark brown hair and hazel eyes.

Phillip built computer systems as a side business. They only worked together for about six months. Near the end of that time, Scott bought a computer from him and took me along to negotiate the price. Phillip was six feet tall with dark curly hair and a deep, seductive voice. He was friendly but came across as a little arrogant. We discussed what it was we wanted the computer for, as he built them to suit the user's needs.

Phillip's office was in the basement of his home. It also served as a work area to build computers. It was a mess. Parts were strewn everywhere, packing materials all over the floor, ashtrays full of cigarette butts. Phillip had what I called a flat-surface syndrome — if there was a flat surface, he had to put something on it.

"How can you work in this mess?" I inquired, as I looked around the room in astonishment.

"This is pretty clean since I knew you two were coming," he replied.

"Hmmm, I do organizational services for businesses. I could come in and set up a system where your workflow, as well as your inventory needs, are considered. The structure will help you work more efficiently. Would you be interested in me helping you?"

"Maybe, what would it cost?"

"I would need to come for about two hours and talk with you about exactly what you do, how you do it and figure out a proposal and cost based on the time it would take."

"Okay, let's set up a time for you to come by. I would be interested in getting a proposal."

"This means that we get a discount on the computer, right?" Scott asked with a grin.

"No," Phillip answered with a laugh.

The following week I went over to meet with Phillip to discuss his business. I was surprised by how open he was; most people hide their messiness and where they have issues. We talked about his strange work schedule, why he shouldn't smoke around computer components and his family. He had been married for almost fifteen years, with a son a few months older than Joshua and daughter, who was six years older than the boys. His wife worked first shift, and he worked third, so she got the kids off to school, and when they got home, he was there. This schedule allowed him to have time with them in the evenings before going to work. The computer business seemed to be a creative outlet for him, as well as an additional source of income for the family.

A few days after the meeting, I sent the proposal to Phillip, who reviewed it with his wife, and they agreed to hire me to get the business organized. In the fall of 1996 — on Phillip's off-days, while Joshua was in preschool — I started working a few hours one day a week, for eight weeks. While I was organizing, cleaning, setting up systems, and filing paperwork, Phillip was talking. He was telling me stories about his kids, his family in Indiana, and his philosophical thinking. Phillip and I didn't agree on many issues; he was, however, an excellent listener. Most people don't know how vital listening is. But he did. He was someone who not only listened to what I had to say but heard me.

At the beginning of January 1997, I was no longer married. Now I was a divorced woman with a young child who needed a job and a place to live. I was fortunate to be very active in a loving church home with caring people. I was taken in by a sweet young couple. I had my teaching certificate, so I started taking substitute teaching jobs at the local schools. And with Phillip's recommendation, I also started to help his clients set up the software on their computers.

Phillip's wife told him in December 1996 that she wanted a

divorce. It was very messy and took until June 1997 before there was an agreement signed. Phillip moved in with another family from the church, which he was now attending regularly. We had become wonderful friends and helped each other when we could and spent much time talking. He learned about my past, and I learned about his trust issues, and we went to church whenever it was open.

During the Fourth of July holiday weekend, my youngest stepbrother was in a car accident. Not wearing his seatbelt, he was ejected from the car and suffered from severe head wounds. I immediately went home to be with the family before he succumbed to his injuries.

To my marvelous surprise, Phillip flew to Pennsylvania to comfort me and attended all the services. He took time off from work without pay. I was in awe that someone stopped their life to comfort me during a challenging time. I realized that, despite the emotionally charged surroundings, in his presence, I wasn't scared. I felt completely safe when I was with him. This feeling was the first time I could remember feeling safe since the visit with my mother when I was eleven. Despite what my head was saying — run away — my heart was telling me I was safe at last. For the first time since the fateful summer visit with my mother, I followed my heart. Thirty days after his divorce was final, Phillip and I married on August 3, 1997, in a small church ceremony with our parents and children present.

Joshua and I moved into Phillip's two-story house, and the three of us settled into a routine once school started. Phillip was unhappy that his two children had to move to California. Although he had shared custody, the kids lived with their mother. They came to visit at Christmas, and we worked together to blend these individuals into a family. We had a game night, we did crafts, and we watched movies together as a family.

Since Phillip had moved to Georgia in 1990, he had always wanted to move back to his hometown of Aurora, Indiana. In April 1998, nine months after we got married, the opportunity for a transfer to that area became available. We had several lengthy discussions about it.

"We would be close to my family," he stated as a pro for the list we were forming to help us with this decision.

"Yes, being close to family is a pro, but it can also be a con," I commented back. "What other pros are there?" I questioned as I sat down at the kitchen table where he was sitting.

"I love the area. We could build our dream house on the land I played on when I was a kid, which my grandmother still owns. It's a small, close-knit community — everyone knows everyone."

"That, too, can be a con," I pointed out. "Other cons are that Joshua would have to leave his dad in Georgia and change schools. You know how upset you were when your kids moved to California."

"Yes, but he still could see his dad every other weekend since he could fly for free as his dad works for an airline. And he may do better in school since the class sizes would be a lot smaller," he countered back.

"Since your kids would be flying in from California, are there direct flights for them to Cincinnati?" I questioned since that was the airport where he'd be stationed.

"Yes, there are direct flights, so no problem there," he replied.

"It's a lot colder there, and it's in Tornado Alley," I said fearfully.

"Yes, but Indiana has all four seasons, and there has never been a tornado in Aurora."

"You want to try to go home again? There's a saying that you can't do it since what you remember growing up is different when you're an adult with a different perspective."

I knew he wanted to go. I would not try to stop the move. A new place for this newly blended family to start fresh was something that seemed reasonable. The list was helpful, but I couldn't come up with a valid reason not to move—it was what he wanted to do.

Phillip moved to Indiana for his April start date. He came back to Georgia on weekends while we sold the house, and Joshua finished out the school year. Joshua was excited about the move even though he would be farther away from his dad. But he would see him every other weekend as he had been. He would just be flying on an airplane to get to Georgia. In June, we packed up everything and moved in with Phillip's parents.

All wounds require time to heal, depending on the severity of the damage. My body had its timetable for healing based on how I was taking care of myself overall—and not just the injury. Outwardly, I appeared to have no issues. I could speak about what occurred in my past calmly. I knew that others could see that I was moving past the hurt and betrayal and hoped it would help them find the courage in themselves to move forward as well.

But I was unaware that there was an issue with the healing process, a festering under the skin, a low-grade fever that I didn't deal with completely. When I started to realize that I was now utterly safe with Phillip, other issues arose. I couldn't deal with anything else if I felt that my safety was in jeopardy. Physiological needs are the lower part of Maslow's Hierarchy of Needs, and my access to food, water, shelter, etc. was always taken care of by my father. Safety is the second level. With Phillip's arrival in my life, I could complete this level of need.

So, once my basic physiological and safety needs were met, I started to realize that how I interacted with others and how I felt about myself were a bit skewed. I realized I was an overachiever and a people pleaser as a way to feel good about myself. I was allowing what others thought about me to be overly influential and to affect how I felt about myself. This realization was when I started to set real boundaries with others.

Our new living situation was not unique and not ideal. Although everyone was happy that we were in Aurora, we all needed more space than this family home provided. Before we were married, Phillip introduced me to his parents, Phil and Nancy, I told them up front that I was very direct. And that if they asked me a question, they might not like my answer. Phillip dubbed this the "sledgehammer of truth." Looking back, I can see that this was a passive way for me to release underlying anger at someone, but to excuse the behavior since I was speaking the truth.

We had been living in Aurora for about six months when things got a bit tense. We were due to move out between Christmas and New Year's into a small rental house while we were building a home on the land Phillip had dreamed about living on since he was little. My new mother-in-law and I were talking, and she asked me a question about a situation she found herself in. I knew she would not like my answer. Nancy didn't and left the room, crying. Although she was upset, I knew she wasn't angry with me. However, I do remember what my new father-in-law did.

"What is Nancy crying?" he shouted at me.

"She asked a question and didn't like the answer I gave her. I am sorry that it upset her, but I did nothing wrong," I stated in my defense.

As he picked up the phone, he said quite calmly, "I am calling the police to have you removed from this house."

At first, I was stunned, but I realized that he was serious when he started dialing the phone.

"You don't have to call the police, and I will be happy to leave this house," I said as I grabbed my purse and called for Joshua to get his coat on.

Joshua and I went to a place at the airport where we could watch the airplanes take off. The lights were quite calming. I called Phillip, who was working, and told him what happened. He, in turn, called his dad, and they fought. A few hours later, my mother-in-law let me into the house after Phillip spoke to her. She apologized for her husband's outburst and behavior, something she did quite often. I told her not to worry about it and that I knew how I needed to handle him. This incident was the conscious start of my setting personal boundaries with others so they couldn't harm me.

During the three weeks, we had to live together, my father-in-law and I were home alone as neither he nor I worked. One afternoon my father-in-law got mad at me and started yelling.

"Dad, your threats mean nothing to me," I responded.

He then dramatically grabbed his chest like he was in pain and leaned back like he was going to fall.

"Go ahead, have a heart attack, see if I care," I said as I stepped away, slamming the door to the basement.

Now, I didn't want any harm to come to this man, but I wasn't going to allow him to manipulate me the way I saw him doing to the rest of his family. I snuck back upstairs to see if he was okay and found him on his computer, smoking a cigarette, perfectly fine. He never tried that manipulation on me again. And, a few weeks later, in December 1998, we had moved out of their home permanently.

The summer of 2000 was when this newly blended family was trying to get used to one another. We also realized that the kids were getting a lot of negativity from the other parent. This situation is sad because this reflects the one doing the negative talking and only harms the children. Barry, Phillip's youngest, who is only three months older than my son Joshua, had been a very affectionate child with me previously. He loved to give hugs and cuddle on the couch while watching television. When Barry came to visit for the summer, something had changed. He seemed to pull back when I went to hug him and did not want to cuddle on the couch anymore. At first, I thought this was him growing up a little, now that Barry was eight years old and didn't want to be treated like a little kid. But when I would go to cuddle with Joshua, he seemed to get sad.

"Barry, do you want to come and sit on the couch with me to watch the movie?" I inquired.

"No, I will sit over here," he replied with a frown on his face.

"Are you sure? We can make room for you on this side of the couch, and one of the puppies can lie on your lap."

The look on his face said yes, but he said, "No, I don't want to watch a movie," and got up and went into the bedroom he shared with Joshua and his sister.

I got up and followed him. "Barry, what's wrong? You're the one that asked if we could watch this movie. You can tell me anything, you know. I won't get mad; I want to help you."

He squirmed a bit as he grabbed his pillow, hugging it before responding, "My mom told me that if I need hugs or if I wanted to cuddle, I had to do it with Sissy and not you."

"Oh, honey, I'm so sorry that you are in a situation like this. I didn't mean to make you feel uncomfortable. You shouldn't feel bad for liking me or wanting to be loved. I love you. I understand that you don't want to disobey your mom, but do you think that she doesn't want other people to love you? That's all that I am trying to do: love and take care of you while you are visiting."

"She said you're not family."

"Well, she is right that she and I aren't family. But your daddy and I are married, and we have brought our children together to form a new, extended family. Not only do you have Sissy, but you also have a new brother, Joshua. My family sees you as part of their family; remember they sent you Christmas gifts? I think a family is a group of people that decide to love one another. What do you think?"

"I guess."

"If your mom decided to get married again, don't you think she would want you to like her new husband? Don't you think that he would want to love and take care of you too?"

"I guess."

"So, how is loving you and taking care of you when you are here different?"

"It's not," he said. Then he slowly rose and came over to hug me, and we all watched the movie together.

My sister moved in with us in the summer of 2001. Tammi asked for shelter from an abusive relationship. Inside me, the tape saying, "take care of your baby sister," kicked on. After speaking with Phillip, I showed up at her house to move her to Indiana with her two children.

After the visit to Alaska with my mother, mom started drinking again, so I didn't speak to her. My mother now had my home phone number so she and Tammi could talk, and since I answered the phone, she would try to have a bit of a conversation with me. Again, I was polite — *honor thy mother* — and would speak to her for a few moments before putting Tammi on the phone. Tammi only stayed the summer before moving back to Pennsylvania, and I didn't have the phone number changed. So, every so often, mom would call. I told her that as long as she was sober, I would speak with her.

Then one afternoon, she called. She was very drunk and furious. I reminded her that I would not speak with her when she was drunk, and I was hanging up the phone when she exploded.

"How dare you hang up on me? I am your mother. I gave birth to you," she shrieked.

Calmly, while clenching my teeth, I said, "Mom, I put boundaries in place so I wouldn't get hurt."

"You hurt — for what? What did I ever do to you? You caused all this grief and pain in my life…" was all I heard as I hung up on her and unplugged the phone.

The next day I had our phone number changed and made it an unlisted number. I also called Tammi to tell her what happened. I told her I would give her my phone number, but she had to promise not to give it to mom, or I would change it again and not give it to her either. She understood and never gave mom my number.

Boundaries seem like punishment to those who receive them, but I put them into place for my own protection like I did with my father-in-law. Setting boundaries is a form of self-care and self-love. This incident was the beginning of self-esteem building within me. The start of me being independent and creating my safe place for dealing with my fears.

I still have wounds. The hurts I haven't healed from for whatever reason. They are the ones that cause me to overreact to situations that no one else reacts to. The unintentional words that a well-meaning person said to me I have taken and warped into something else. Then I replay it repeatedly, like my mental tape playing in my head to "*take care of your baby sister.*" Or my wounds are the big ones that I do not know how to get over, including child molestation, rape, abandonment, physical abuse, emotional abuse, psychological abuse.

These wounds are ones that I have hidden under a protective blanket. The ones I let few people see. These sores are the ones that fewer people know. At times, I have realized that these lesions are oozing and infected. I began to understand that the protective blanket I was using had sprouted thorns from old defense mechanisms. It was no longer benefiting me, but was now causing me harm.

As I made my way through life, I started to feel that the blanket was becoming too heavy for me to carry all the time. It had been weighed down over time with additional wounds and scar tissue. I knew this security blanket had helped me and, in many ways, protected me. I thought about being brave and shedding it. As I tried to take it off, there was an unfamiliar pain, a hurt that surprised me. This newfangled hurt was the discomfort of healing. All wounds tingle when they heal, even emotional injuries. This new aching wasn't something I wanted to deal with, so I put the thorny blanket back on. I tried to continue walking through life with the weight on my shoulders, but I realized that I didn't have to carry it anymore.

The unfamiliar pain was no different. It was part of the healing process. As with any wound, it needed to see the light. It needed to breathe. As I took off the thorny blanket, I needed to realize that this act of self-care was an act of self-love and a step in my healing process. Yet, I struggled to get past this step. This unfamiliar pain was unfamiliar, and it was something different I had to learn to handle. The thorny blanket, however, was familiar agony. Despite it being painful, at least I knew what it was and how to not deal with it.

Only when I honestly couldn't bear the load of the thorny blanket, did I decide that I must take it off. And only then could I truly heal from my wounds. Yes, there is a unique type of pain that I needed to become accustomed to, but now the sores could truly heal.

When I had finally realized that I could no longer carry my thorny blanket, I stripped it off like a bandage—as fast as I could—thinking it would be less painful. I am not sure if that was the case or not, but I quickly realized that I had more oozing sores than I initially thought. Although I courageously and consciously felt the blanket was taken off, I soon recognized that this would be a process that took time. One that needed me to analyze each of the seeping spots more carefully for them to heal.

At the age of thirty-one, I had been out of therapy for almost 15 years. When we moved to Indiana, I was no longer part of a tight-knit church community. Other than Phillip, who is my best friend, I had no one else to help me deal with these wounds. So, I spent much time staying busy, thinking if I stayed busy, the healing process would occur on its own. Some may see this as avoidance or procrastination. But at the time, I thought this was a way to force me to learn to deal with others. By surrounding myself with people, I didn't know I could learn a fresh approach to interact with them and make healthy connections.

The sledgehammer of truth that I would wield needed to be put away for a while. I needed to learn tactfulness. I needed to start believing that these new people in my life didn't want to hurt me. I needed to understand that people naturally come into and leave our lives, and this is not abandonment. My son growing up and starting his own life is natural and does not mean he is choosing to abandon me.

God used what was around me for my awakening as well as for

my growth. The church was a marvelous place to begin my understanding of God and learning about the scriptures. But after we moved, I realized that some of us outgrow the church community. I developed an awareness that I'm responsible for my spiritual growth, my return to my authentic self. I was still studying the Bible through a non-denominational organization called the Bible Study Fellowship. I also began to read other books on spiritual growth, by authors such as Marianne Williamson, Gary Zukav, and Eckhart Tolle. They kindled the fire of growth that was developing within me.

In Indiana, when I was away from everyone who had perceptions of me, I was able to nurture myself. I was able to overcome the codependent tendencies, let go of some fear-based reactions to circumstances, and blossom back into the independent girl I once was. I started to come into myself. I was trying unique ways of presenting myself, determining what I liked and what was useful.

By the summer of 2001, I was a confident speaker, trainer, and leader for the local Cub Scout Pack, which led me into the District Team. There I became the Day Camp Director for three years, as well as the head of the Scouting Roundtable. Through these positions, I reframed my obsessive control issues into outstanding organizational skills to create programs that helped the leaders. It also gave the boys a fun learning experience. I started seeing that parts of me that could be seen as unfavorable could also be constructive. I was able to reframe my thinking and how I saw myself.

CHAPTER 5 CALMING THE MIND AND SEEING THE PAST DOESN'T HAVE TO REPEAT ITSELF

WE ALL GROW OUT OF OUR EXPERIENCES

Raven quiets the voice of the ego,

To listen to the Spirit, she has forgotten.

~Calm

~Peaceful

~Whole

~Creative

Light has returned.

Phillip worked in the airline industry and had a good source of income for me to be able to stay at home to care for the family. After 9/11, we had a tough time financially. He was laid off from the job that he had for fifteen years, and job prospects in the industry were nonexistent.

I had a friend, Vicki, living in Georgia, who had organization issues. She would pay me to visit and help her organize her business. So, after the layoff, she convinced me that we should move back down south and help her with the school she was running. I had no doubts that this was the right decision and convinced Phillip that we should move.

In the summer of 2005, Joshua, Barry, and I moved into Vicki's large home, where she lived with her two boys. Phillip stayed in Indiana to prepare the house for selling. After a few weeks, he joined us despite the residence not being sold. While I was helping to run the business and household, Phillip was fixing all the broken items in both areas. Because we were living with her, and she wasn't charging us for room and board, she didn't pay us for helping with the business.

Vicki had a talent for making money. She would go and collect unwanted kittens and then sell them for $20 each. Vicki sold a dog for $400 that had been given to her because it chewed the wood chairs of a dining room suite. She told the buyers about the chewing issue and made it sound like it was a cute behavior. She did, however, have problems with paying her bills and always seemed to need money. Her unorganized accounting resulted in me handling the household and business finances. I took care of the bills and kept the household on a budget.

I was enjoying having a girlfriend again. Vicki had a rough childhood and experienced much verbal abuse in her first marriage, so there was a part of her that doubted her innate abilities. We helped build each other's self-esteem, so we had a shared bond of overcoming our past. We would plan meals, buy groceries, and cook together. We drove into work together, and the boys all played well with each other. As long as Vicki and I were together, everything seemed to be all right.

"Why don't you blame your dad for what happened in New Mexico?" she asked while driving us to work one morning.

"It wasn't his fault. He couldn't have predicted or prevented what happened," I responded.

"Sure, he did. He knew your mom was an alcoholic. He knew she couldn't be trusted, especially since you would be so far away."

I sat dumbfounded by the statement that I never considered. It was true. Daddy knew mom better than anyone. He shouldn't have allowed us to go 1,500 miles away and be alone with her.

Why hadn't I ever thought about this before?

"Your dad didn't protect you, and he should have. Why aren't you upset with him?" She pushed for a reaction.

"My dad did try to cancel our visit, but I'm the one that convinced him to let Tammi and I go."

"He was the adult, and you were the child. He shouldn't have let you go no matter what you said. He should have protected you from her. He didn't do his job."

We sat in silence for the rest of the drive. At the age of thirty-six, in the twenty-five years since the traumatic event, I had never blamed my father for the abuse. It never even dawned on me that he did anything wrong. Had I not considered Vicki, a close friend, I think I would have dismissed it. But instead, I allowed my egoic mind, which likes to blame, to take over my thinking.

Later that day, as this new line of thoughts consumed my mind, I realized that I had released blame concerning the events that occurred in New Mexico. I was no longer a victim looking to blame others for my current situation. I was a survivor who took responsibility for her actions. Therefore, I couldn't place blame on my father now for a decision that he made over twenty-five years before. I'm sure that he has many regrets concerning that visit. Still, I wasn't going to go backward on my overcoming journey because of what Vicki said to me.

During this time of financial stress and moving back to Georgia, Phillip's son Barry decided he wanted to live with us. He was now 14 years old, and, in the state of Georgia, which had the legal venue, he was allowed to choose with which parent he wanted to live. So, we got an attorney and filed the paperwork. Although Phillip had paid child support, he did not request it from Barry's mother, hoping she wouldn't try to fight this in court. She agreed to the new custody arrangement, and Barry was now permanently living with us.

About a month after school started, Phillip and I were alone, which was now a rarity since we had three adults and four teenage boys living under one roof. He wanted to talk to me about the influence that Vicki had on me.

"Why do you believe everything she tells you?" he inquired while pacing back and forth.

"I don't think I do," I replied defensively, "but I have known her for over 15 years, I trust her opinion."

"She has you upset with your dad because he allowed you to go visit your mother when you were eleven. You weren't upset with him before talking to her."

"Well, I hadn't thought about the fact that he should've known better and not allowed me to go."

As I said this, I realized that he was right. Never once was I upset with my dad over the past two decades. I hadn't ever thought my dad did anything wrong because he hadn't. But all of a sudden, Vicki was influencing me in ways I didn't realize, and I wasn't too fond of it. Why was I allowing her opinions to change how I felt about my past or people she didn't know? As I listened to Phillip, I realized that he was scared.

"Don't you see, she's trying to pull you away from me?" he cried. "I love you, but I can't get you to even listen to me anymore. I don't want to lose you, and I feel I am."

"I'm sorry, I didn't realize I was making you feel this way. I'm not leaving you. I love you, and I should listen to what you have to say, even if I don't like it. You're my husband, and your perspective is different but valuable. I need to hear what you have to say."

After this conversation, things changed concerning my

relationship with Vicki. Although we worked together, I spent less time with her and more time with Phillip and the boys, which seemed to disappoint her. I also put an end to talking with her about my dad, as well as my past. I told her I wanted to focus on the present. She started to be a little bit passive-aggressive with me in her comments about what I wanted. She would outright disagree with me in front of her employees, which she never did before. Our friendship was changing quickly.

We'd been back in Georgia for over three months, living with Vicki, and with both Phillip and I working for her business. We had an understanding that our compensation for working for the company was room, board, and money to pay the mortgage payment we still had since the Indiana house hadn't sold yet. Phillip was fixing items in her home along with her vehicles, without getting compensated for his services. But when we paid our mortgage payment for the second month, she decided mortgage payments were no longer part of the deal, and she wanted that money back.

All of us in the household attended a rather large and renowned non-denominational church. Vicki and I agreed that we would take this dispute to them to resolve, as was suggested in the Bible. We went to meet with one of the assistant pastors and explained the problem, but he said that it was a legal matter, and the church couldn't get involved. Vicki and I were astounded. We both agreed to sign a legal waiver, so the church couldn't be held liable. But this assistant pastor still wouldn't help us and wouldn't even take it to the head pastor or the deacons to discuss.

So, to maintain peace, I paid Vicki the money she wanted. This misunderstanding ended what I thought, at the time, was a friendship. Phillip, Barry, Joshua, and I moved out of her house the following week into a rental property she owned. We both got jobs as soon as we could, and, by November, we had removed ourselves from her life.

In less than six months, our lives changed completely. We were now renting an 800-square-foot, double-wide trailer with two teenage boys. I was working full time for the first time in Joshua's life. We didn't have money for internet or cable so we couldn't watch TV. Yet we were happy. We took joy in the simple things. We all read books in the evening and still had a game night. Being together was what mattered.

In January of 2006, Phillip and I realized that we couldn't keep up the payments on the debt we had and provide for the boys on the salaries we now received. Therefore, we declared bankruptcy. I was so against this and struggled with the decision. I was ashamed of not being able to pay the bills. I felt guilty, as we got into this mess through my so-called friend.

Phillip was very logical about the decision. He reminded me that some of the liability he had was due to his willingness to take a large part of the debt he and his first wife accumulated. Phillip kept reminding me that the economic issues the airlines faced were inevitable after 9/11, which caused his furlough. He explained that this was the best choice for the family since we now had both boys living with us.

It was amazing how being released from that debt was so life-altering. We were now able to save up for a deposit on a more suitable rental property for the four of us to live in, where the boys had separate rooms. We had extra money so the boys could participate in extracurricular activities at school. Life became a bit easier.

Since I had a problem with the leadership of the church we were going to, I didn't want to attend. This issue with the church caused great angst within me and my household because Phillip liked that church. So, we continued to go until we moved far enough away that Phillip didn't want to make the drive three times a week.

I understood that people aren't perfect, but I still saw the world in black and white. What the leadership of that church did was wrong, and I couldn't reconcile it in my mind. I still believed in God, I still had my faith placed correctly, but the church was different. I could now see why so many people left the church because of wounds the people within the church caused others.

It's sad that the institution that is supposed to support the wounded and the hopeless causes so much harm. I know there are lovely congregations out there, I have been a part of many. Still, I also understand the pain that can be caused by strict adherence to man's rules and false tenets. God meets us where we are, and He met me here in this place of doubt and change.

Phillip and I have high-end digital cameras, and he started driving me around the area. We drove into the North Georgia mountains and took pictures of the beauty of nature. Here is where God met me, His natural world. We can find Him in every aspect of His creation. The time Phillip and I spent doing this was a time of renewal for us as a couple and for me reconnecting with nature.

We have some fantastic photographs of the wonders we discovered during these times. I found myself immersed in the beauty and the simplicity of nature. The unassuming sound of water trickling in a creek. The blossoming of a simple white daisy on a sunny afternoon. The cow in a field walking down the hill to get its picture taken.

Here in the countryside, I remembered the silence I found in the storm drain in Maryland. I was able to hear myself reflect on what had taken place over the past turbulent year and know that everything was working out. We were okay. I was loved and supported. Despite what was happening all around me, all was well, and peace started to creep into my life when I would get quiet.

One night in the spring of 2006, Tammi called unexpectedly. She was crying.

"Mom's in the hospital and is unconscious. She listed you as the person to make medical decisions for her. Please don't let her die," she whimpered.

"What's wrong with her?" I asked in a bit of shock. Why on earth would she choose me to handle her medical decisions when we haven't spoken in years? Tammi should be the one to deal with this.

"The hospital won't tell me. They said they could only speak to you. I have a phone number for you to call. Please don't let mom die," she implored.

"Tammi, I will call and do what I can," I said hesitantly. I hung up with her and called the hospital. The nurse said that her tuberculosis had returned, and she was having a difficult time breathing. They needed permission to treat, which I gave.

Mom was in the hospital for eight weeks. I would call each week to speak to the doctor or nurse about her condition, and inform Tammi of her progress. It was a strange feeling to be taking care of my mother again after all these years. I didn't want to be involved, but she dragged me into this odd relationship. I also did it for Tammi. I didn't want her to think that I would let mom die because of our painful past.

Her last week in the hospital, she asked to speak to me. I knew she was sober, so I agreed. It was a short but enlightening conversation.

"Hi, baby, how are you?" she asked timidly, despite her hoarseness.

"Well, thank you. Are you feeling better?"

"Yes. Thank you for handling the healthcare decisions for me when I was unconscious."

"You're welcome. Mom, why did you pick me? It should've been Tammi."

"No, baby, you're the oldest," she quickly responded. "I'm glad you agreed to speak with me. I know you've been hurt and are upset with me."

I sat back onto the bed, stunned by what I heard. Did my mother just acknowledge what happened in New Mexico? "What are you talking about, mom?"

"The rape," she softly whispered as she hung up the phone.

I lay on the bed for a while, crying, not understanding what happened. Was mom admitting her part in the rape, or just that she knew the event occurred? I would never know for sure.

After being released from the hospital, mom went to visit Tammi. She had Tammi call me. "Hi, baby, how are you?"

"I'm fine. How are you feeling? Did you have a good bus trip across the country?" I asked, thinking about our bus ride from Pennsylvania to New Mexico all those years before.

"I'm feeling good. I have more trouble breathing since I started smoking again. I'm enjoying the time with my grandkids and seeing your sister."

"If you stay sober, Joshua and I may come up to visit," I said cautiously.

"Really?"

"If you stay sober, yes." She ended the conversation quickly. Two days later, I called Tammi, and she told me mom was drinking again, so we didn't visit.

I wasn't surprised but disappointed. Then I thought maybe mom's anxiety of seeing me caused her to relapse. Here went my egoic mind trying to make me responsible for the actions of my mother. I never spoke to her again. A few weeks later, she was on her way to Alaska. She and Tammi spoke once in a while, but she never did reach out to me.

As the boys went through high school, we settled into a comfortable routine. Phillip and I worked, and whoever got home first started dinner. Just like when my dad remarried, we always ate dinner together each night. We made sure the boys had homework completed and whatever they needed for school. We split the holidays with the other parents, so Phillip and I had some time to ourselves.

Phillip has owned a Honda Gold Wing motorcycle since we got married. We took a few weekend trips in Indiana but didn't ride much. Since the boys needed us around less, we decided to find a local group of Gold Wing riders to learn the area. So, I found a local chapter of the Gold Wing Road Riders Association (GWRRA, a national organization) that was meeting near us, and we went. Phillip and I had looked online, and they needed someone to help with upkeep for the website and the monthly newsletter. We thought we could volunteer for those positions. When we arrived, we discovered that it was the chapter's last meeting because they couldn't find anyone to be the chapter directors.

At the end of the meeting, I went up to pay the membership fee for the national organization. I was speaking to the assistant district director. "What does the chapter director do?" I inquired as I was writing the check.

"Well, it means that you are responsible for holding the monthly gatherings. You have a monthly outing of some kind where the members can get together to ride and report these items to the Georgia State district director," he responded.

"Is there training and support provided?"

"Yes, there's a complete training program, and I'll be here to help you out as best I can. I can't be the chapter director as well as assist on the district team."

Phillip was returning from the bathroom, and I said, "Sign this, please," and he did. Phillip handed the document to the assistant director.

"Congratulations," he said excitedly, "you are now the chapter director for Georgia Chapter D of the GWRRA!"

"What?" Phillip questioned as he turned to look at me.

"Well, we were going to be webmaster and newsletter editor. We don't want the chapter to close, so I thought we could do it. It'll be fun!" I smiled coyly at him. In June 2008, we were leading a biker gang!

Phillip was a bit stunned at first, but not surprised. The following week we visited two other chapters to see how a monthly gathering functioned. The national convention was a week later in South Carolina. We went with a few chapter members, but our goal was to get the training that we needed. Instead, the head of education for the Southern region wouldn't hold any teachings for six months. I was livid. No wonder the organization had issues finding or keeping volunteers to hold positions when they didn't know how to ensure success.

So, on a long car trip, I read the manuals I had downloaded from the internet out loud to Phillip. From these two handbooks, I planned out the rest of the year's activities. I looked for people to hold the other open positions, and soon we had a growing active chapter. Within a year, we had participated in more events and won more awards than any other chapter in the state. Every weekend we were riding somewhere with our little biker gang. Whether we were going to a District-sponsored occasion, a ride in the countryside, or an overnight trip, we were busy.

Without realizing it, weekly activities filled our calendar, and our sweet routine life ended. I spent evenings planning events, sending out reminder emails, and creating the monthly newsletter. We went from a roster of 110 members to over 300 members in five years. We had again taken a small group and enlarged its scope, like with the Cub Scout pack, and we had a great time with our new friends. We took the leadership course, rider education courses, and soon became instructors for the National organization.

As I look back over my life, it's easy to see the pattern I kept repeating. Whenever my life seemed to calm down, when I was able to focus on healing myself, I found something to keep me very distracted. Staying busy is also known as being a workaholic; the compulsive need to work for long hours. Staying physically or mentally busy kept my mind from dealing with the underlying issues that caused pain. Workaholism looked like reading into the wee hours of the morning, so I didn't have to go to sleep because when I tried, my mind went to a fearful place, and I didn't know what to do. Although keeping busy helped me for a period, I had to come face to face with the pain; it's the only way to overcome it.

I spent decades staying busy. I started as a full-time college student taking eighteen credit hours and working thirty-five hours a week at Sears & Roebuck. Full time was not just two semesters; it was all year. I finished my bachelor's degree in social sciences in three years. The only breaks I had were when there were no classes scheduled. When I married Scott, within the first year I was working full time, we were building a house, and I had a baby.

When Joshua started preschool, I started volunteering. I volunteered to co-teach a Sunday school class. I volunteered to lead Vacation Bible School for three years. And when I do something, I don't do it just a little—I overdo it. VBS attendance grew each year that I was the director. Let's not forget all the Cub Scouting activities we were involved in—leading the pack, day camp director for three years, district roundtable coordinator.

All of this was fun, productive, helpful, and beneficial for all involved—except for me. I was using all this activity, productiveness, and helpfulness to keep me from looking at myself. My ego was using these delightful things as distractions from healing my wounds.

When I realized the pattern of my behavior, I started asking many questions. Why was I spending so much of my free time volunteering? What was I getting from it? Frustration, yes, but more importantly, self-worth? Staying busy doing good things for others is a great way not to take the time to work on yourself. I have always been introspective, and since we were riding every weekend, I spent much time on the back of the bike thinking. Riding in the mountains on a lovely day observing the natural beauty all around can be very peace-inducing. Again, Spirit always met me where I was. Amongst the biker gang, I found friendship, teachers, fun, students, mentees, and new acquaintances who all helped me become a better person.

I didn't think I was good enough just as I was, and I kept comparing myself to others. Comparison is something we all do. Society is quick to analyze everything and determine who is more worthy. In my journal, I compared my capabilities, or lack thereof, with those who were so much more talented than I believed I ever could be. Am I good enough? How did I define my worthiness?

Let me clearly state, right now, that you are good enough, and I am good enough because we were born as unique individuals. No one else on this planet is like me, so I can't compare myself to anyone. I may be similar to others. Some may like to paint, but not the way I paint. I may like sci-fi movies, but I have different favorites than my husband does. I, just being authentically me, am good enough. No more, no less. My incorrect thinking about my worthiness came from my mother.

When I was a teenager, my mother told me that I wasn't strong enough and that if I were left alone in the woods, I wouldn't survive. This comment was her version of saying that I wasn't good enough. When she told me this, it made me angry. Still, I didn't realize until years later that I kept playing this tape recording in my head every time I found myself in a tough situation. I wouldn't survive; I wasn't good enough to take care of myself. I wasn't worthy. I didn't have confidence in myself.

Guess what; I am still here! Therefore, I have proven, time and time again, that I am a survivor despite what my mother had told me. Yet, decades later, this still comes up, so why haven't I let it go? Why don't I realize that what she said was wrong? Why do I question my worthiness?

I do know that I am a survivor and that I am good enough, but my ego likes to remind me what my mother said over thirty years ago. The ego is the keeper of my negative tape recordings, which comes out as negative self-talk. For some reason, it doesn't keep records of all the ways I have proven that I am good enough, just those times I have failed at something. Thus substantiating, I'm not worthy.

It became necessary for me to reframe my life. What I mean by this is, I needed to honestly evaluate my long-held beliefs to determine if they were still things I believed. Or, maybe, now that I see a different perspective, those beliefs are no longer valid.

The first thing I needed to reframe in my life was to modify my self-talk. I realized that my ego programmed my inner voice. By developing positive self-talk, it was easier to reframe my story.

I appraised the narrative I'd been telling myself and became aware of the negative aspects it created in my life. Therefore, I began to change how I spoke to myself. I needed to talk to myself with self-care and a growth mindset. The self-talk allowed me to construct the life I always imagined.

I knew, on a surface level, that words can be cruel because they have power. I've been hurt by what someone has said to me. I know that words have staying power. I carry wounds from my youth where someone said something to me or called me a name, and it still makes me twinge now when I think about it.

Negativity more easily comes from the ego than something encouraging does. My egoic mind is my worst critic. The things I said to myself are far worse than I'd ever spoken to another. Things like I wasn't smart enough, pretty enough, or that I wasn't worthy of love. Replaying the tapes that my mother said to me like I wasn't a survivor, I was to blame for her alcoholism, or that I was the reason her marriage ended. I find it amazing that the worst suffering I endured since the traumatic visit to New Mexico all occurred within my mind, inflicted by the negative words I spoke to myself. So, to alter this paradigm, I needed to understand how I use words and change my mindset to use them positively.

I've been guilty of using my words as weapons against another, as the ego finds ways to hurt others who have wounded me. Most of these wounds by others are more about their bruised egos than they are about me, but my egoic mind won't let it go. So, I spew back more insults and demeaning phrases for my ego to feel better. This ploy of the ego helps nothing and only perpetuates more negativity.

As time passed, this process got more intense as I thought I had more at stake. I used more sophisticated and politically correct terminology as I aged, but the same negative connotations remained. By tearing down another, the ego falsely inflates itself. But I knew that the opposite was true. Name-calling or labeling others belittles me, not them. It shows my small-mindedness and the innate fear in me.

I was relentless in the amount of badgering I did to myself. Here again, my ego was instilling fear by being the loudest voice in my head. If, however, I got quiet, I heard another influence.

This whisper was the utterance of my soul, our heart voice. This whisper was always present and speaking to me, but I didn't hear it over the screams of my ego. I had to get silent and calm for me to listen to the powerfully positive truth statements from my soul. This place is where my self-talk needs to stem from, this absolute reality from deep within myself.

This place is the part of me that says I can do it; I need to work a little more. My heart believes in my innate abilities. The soul knows the right answers to all the questions my mind asks. But, I have to get silent to hear it speaking to me. I need for it to be the voice I hear encouraging me to move forward past the obstacle in my way because I'm empowered to overcome.

Failure is not a condemnation, and it says nothing about whether or not I am good enough. Disappointment is proof that I'm a survivor. It shows that I'm willing to take risks and try new things. Frustration illustrates my courageous nature. Regret demonstrates that I'm brave for taking the chance. Failure confirms my resilience and therefore is evidence that I'm good enough. I am worthy.

Expectations are those things others may impose upon me or, more likely, I impose on myself. These hopes, when they don't become realities, are the failures my ego uses to cut me down.

These self-inflicted wounds are the so-called proof my ego uses to tell me that I'm not good enough. Again, it's a lie. I know it's a lie, but I struggle because it screams and shouts at me.

The truth, when I pause, take a deep breath and look deep within my authentic self, is that I do know I'm enough. As I try my best in all I do, I realize that my best is enough. Doing my best in every situation is an antidote to disappointment. Because when things don't turn out as I want, I still can gain from the circumstances. By learning from my missteps, I retain my value because I know I'll do better next time. Sitting on the back of the bike in silence, I was able to hear my heart speaking to me. As I listened to it, new areas for me to grow rose up.

The biker gang loved to eat, and there wasn't a Dairy Queen we didn't stop at for ice cream. After a long day of riding, especially on an overnight trip, when we had parked the bikes for the night, various members brought the alcohol out to relax and enjoy the camaraderie.

As a child of an alcoholic, fear still had a hold on my life despite my feeling safe with Phillip. From the years before my parents divorced, I don't have many memories of my mother, where she didn't have a glass of liquor nearby. For two decades, I didn't partake in any alcohol for fear that I would become an alcoholic. I stayed away from all liquor and people who drank it. I didn't want to be around those who could become drunk because they were mean and hurtful — or so I assumed because that is how my mother was. I would get anxious at events with alcohol, especially when the anger would come spewing out of those who were drunk.

I learned from a very young age the signs to look for, so I wasn't in the line of fire when the next violent episode occurred. And, as a child, the feared incident always happened. Consequently, I became conditioned to react to these indications: stumbling, slurred words, angry tone.

I did an excellent job avoiding alcohol and those who drank it, even casually, for years. Then I married Phillip, who was a social drinker. At first, I thought it didn't bother me. With his encouragement, I learned that I did like to drink if I couldn't taste the alcohol. He called these "froufrou drinks" — yummy strawberry daiquiris and what we named chocolate milk, which was Kahlua and cream.

Meanwhile, I was now socially drinking with the biker gang, and that meant I was around more people partaking in alcohol. They would drink and I would realize how uncomfortable I was in these gatherings. I was having a good time with these people, but I kept waiting for someone to get upset and angry. I had to learn that not everyone drinks to excess. Not everyone drinks to escape their past or to forget some pain. Some people drink to relax and enjoy themselves. Could I be one of these people?

Since I only drank cocktails where I couldn't taste the alcohol, I would forget how many I had. I had been tipsy a few times where I felt funny, but I still could think clearly. One night I had a Wallaby Darn at Outback Steakhouse before my salad arrived and a second one before my steak arrived. I finished the third with dessert. Unbeknownst to me, I was drunk, and I was dumbfounded when I had trouble standing up. I also realized as Phillip got me to the car that I was not feeling myself. I was dizzy, and my thoughts were spinning in my head. I went on a verbal tirade on why anyone would want to feel like this — out of control of one's mind and emotions.

This episode scared me. Maybe I could become an alcoholic like my mother? As it turns out, alcohol makes me flirty and then puts me to sleep, rather than making me mean and nasty the way she was. After this incident, I was much more careful about drinking in public. I made sure I had only a sip or two before my meal came, and I only ordered liquor if Phillip was with me.

Out of the blue, I realized that even at home, when it was just the two of us enjoying a hard apple cider together, I would be anxious. I guess I was waiting for Phillip to react negatively and get mean, even though when he has more than enough whiskey, he starts to tell stories. He is a big teddy bear. So why was I still getting fearful when someone near me was drinking?

I am a very logical person. I can see the case for those who drink casually with friends to relax on the weekend. But once you are past the tipsy phase into being drunk, I don't understand why anyone would want to feel that way. My mother was a functional alcoholic. She held down a job with one company for over twenty years, but she never faced her past or her fears due to her addiction. I realized that the little girl inside me was afraid that I was still around her.

All traumas I went through as a child are more difficult to overcome due to the inability of my childlike minds to deal with the situations I was put in. Subsequently, my inner child saw alcohol and prepared herself for nastiness. I would do this even though my adult-self knew the truth could be so different than what I had previously experienced. Alcohol was not the problem; my mother not dealing with her life was the problem. Alcohol was what she chose as her way of hiding from her reality.

Consequently, I realized that my angst with alcohol was my problem, not anyone else's. I needed to take responsibility for my state of mind. My inner child was reacting to something from her past that had no bearing on the present. Therefore, I had to let go of the fear that someone would be unkind. I was no longer a trapped child trying to hide from her cruel, drunk mother. I was an adult, and if I was uncomfortable around anyone drinking, I could easily remove myself from the situation. By being accountable for my emotions, I was able to teach the little girl that not everyone uses alcohol as her mother did. Not everyone drinks to excess. Not everyone is mean and nasty when they choose to partake.

I began to see real-world evidence based on my own observation that just because bad things have happened in the past doesn't mean more bad things will happen. Slurred speech or stumbling from another person doesn't mean that person will cause me harm. Therefore, I can determine the past doesn't have to repeat itself.

Although this took time for me to realize, it doesn't have to. Although my past shaped me, the good news is, I'm not bound to it. I can move past the difficulties of the past and into something far better. The main reason I don't have to repeat history is that I can learn from it.

The biker gang's festive drinking helped me to improve my angst with the issues I had with alcohol. What I experienced as a child was traumatic, mainly because I didn't know how to deal with the situation at the time, and I didn't have options. As an adult, I can always leave circumstances that I find uncomfortable. I chose to stay with the gang and enjoy everyone's company and didn't partake very often, and everything was fine.

Through these newfound friendships, my horizons were expanding. I was traveling all over the South and meeting all kinds of people, and every one of them had something to teach me if I was willing to learn. Ian and Anna taught me to loosen up and have fun. I learned that my angst with alcohol was my issue, and no one else's. Connie, Bubba, and John helped me to deal with personality quirks. Buddy and Charlie exposed me to different leadership styles that both worked. Robin showed me enough, personally created drama that I wanted to keep drama out of my life. Carlos and Julie demonstrated how the thought of losing power or influence could cause jealousy and ultimately cause a downfall. Sharon and Susan verified how laughter could make any day better. Ronnie showed me how powerful silence could be.

The biker gang had a considerable influence on me for many years. We all grow out of our experiences, and we outgrow people, so we have the need to move on. I have a hard time giving up something I feel responsible for, but then there are times that the Universe intervenes on our behalf. In 2012, Phillip was rehired by Delta Airlines and was put on rotating shifts. He couldn't participate with the biker gang, as he was working weekends. So, we slowly backed out of our leadership roles.

It also helped that we kept moving farther and farther away from where the gatherings occurred. After six years of total immersion, we were no longer participating with the biker gang. We have stayed in touch with a few of the members, through social media. People come and go in our lives, and this is a normal process. I needed to allow it to occur so that I could move forward with my growth.

During my adult life, I have been fortunate to be around professionals who taught me how to use a weapon. State police officers and military personnel first trained me, in my early twenties, to handle a pistol. Phillip has owned handguns as well as rifles. Although they were locked up, I didn't particularly care for them. I thought that they were dangerous and knew that I wouldn't use one to hurt anyone, even if threatened. Phillip and I would have discussions about how a pistol lying on the coffee table would never hurt anyone unless a person picked it up and fired it. He concealed carried regularly.

One Saturday morning, I had gone out to do some shopping. As I was coming out of the store, I noticed that two young men from opposite directions began following me to my car. I made it safely to the vehicle, where Phillip had forgotten his pistol. I lifted it and moved it to the passenger seat so the two men could see it. They did, and they both ran off. Later that week, the newspaper reported that a gang was grabbing women from the parking lot and raping them as part of a gang initiation. The realization that I was a target for violence was compelling. I was very thankful that Phillip accidentally left the pistol in my car that day.

That week I applied for my conceal-carry permit. Once I received it, I joined a women's group at the firing range to learn to use the weapon safely and adequately. I spent several months looking for the right pistol for me to own. I wanted one that I was comfortable shooting and one that I could handle alone. The lesson I learned through this experience was that I was capable of taking care of myself. Even in a dangerous situation, I could learn the skills I needed to help me overcome fear and protect myself.

I'm more than proficient with the weapon and was asked to become a National Rifle Association instructor, which I declined. Despite the enjoyment I had with the ladies, I didn't want to spend my time learning additional skills and spend more time involved in the organizational aspects of a group. I realized that this was a test the Universe was giving me to see if I was able to say no when asked for assistance—and I was. In the biker gang, every time I was asked to help in some way, I did. So, I ended up doing the work of many—chapter director, the newsletter editor, district events coordinator, district trainer, national trainer, and drill team coordinator. I was flattered that they asked, but let them know that my time was already committed.

In April of 2011, an unplanned blessing entered my life. On the 24th of the month, Madeliyne Alexandria, my granddaughter, was born. I had known since I was sixteen years old that I would not have a daughter of my own. It was an inner knowing. This awareness knew I was born into a long line of women on my mother's side that was sexually abused, and I recognized that it stopped with me. I discerned that I would be the one to break the cycle by the growth and lessons I was learning.

When Joshua told me that he was going to be a father soon after graduation, I was a bit stunned. I had my hopes and dreams for him, but now he had to deal with things he wasn't ready to handle. I did what I could to support him and the mother, despite the emotions we were all going through.

I was there the day Madeliyne was born. I went to visit her regularly when she was a baby and, when she was three years old, she came on her first overnight with me. Since then, she has been visiting twice a month. We're creative in the studio or the garden. Phillip and I take her on vacation with us to the mountains and the beach, her favorite place.

It's incredible how much she resembles me when I was a toddler. There are pictures of me as a little girl hanging in our home, and she tells me they are pictures of her. She mimics my mannerisms and helps me to put fun into my life. She's my girl, and we have a lot of enjoyable times together.

Her birthday is the day before my mother's. I was hoping that they wouldn't share a birthday. I wanted her day to be separate from all my memories of my mom. She also looks very much like my mother when my mom was a little girl. At first, this surprised me, but I realized that my mother and I look more alike than I believed. I have old photographs that my mother sent me from her family in Alaska. When I look at them, I see myself in her very round face. I see the same sadness in her eyes that was in mine.

Madeliyne came into the world, and my mother left this world a year later, unbeknownst to anyone. She died alone in a state hospital in New Mexico. My sister Tammi and I thought she was in Alaska. She had told the hospital personnel that she didn't have any family, and it took the state two months to find my sister in Pennsylvania. I handled the paperwork with the state to have her cremated, and we sent the ashes to my aunt.

When I completed the paperwork for the state, I realized that I never got the closure or the reconciliation that I had wanted. I thought I needed closure, but in reality, I wanted confirmation of the wrong that was done to me by her. She did acknowledge the sexual abuse the last time we spoke on the phone in 2006. And ultimately, she abandoned herself at the end. Maybe that was her way of acknowledging the abandonment of her two little girls on the rough streets of Albuquerque.

Reconciliation was the hope I held onto for thirty-three years. Loving her wasn't the problem; I did love her. It's why I wouldn't allow any finality in the personal boundaries I put into place to help protect me from her drunken, hateful outbursts. No child wants to be at odds with a parent for most of their lives. Despite the closeness we had before my parents divorced, I spent most of my life feeling detached from any understanding of my mother.

I can look over her life, or at least the parts that I was aware of, and feel sorry for her. She went through a lot as a child in a sustenance life eight miles inside the arctic circle with no running water or electricity. Being given up for adoption and having to enter an unknown world while giving up her culture. Then marrying a man on his way to Vietnam who didn't believe he was returning. After divorcing my father, she was raped and abused by others. She didn't have ways to cope with what she didn't understand, so she tried to bury it with alcohol and then drugs.

I don't think she ever was able to bury the past enough that she wasn't in pain or turmoil. And maybe at some point, her conscience got the better of her, and she drank to hide the suffering she caused my sister and me. I don't know. I know that I was sad that she died alone and sad she died before we could reconcile.

CHAPTER 6 EVERYDAY MIRACLES

EMPOWERMENT IS THE REWARD FOR SUCCESSFUL ACTION

Grandmother Moon at the start of the day

Smiling down upon the Earth;

To help Raven remember that all is well,

that it will be a great day;

If she is aware of the miracles that are always present.

In 2014, after nine years of living in rental houses, Phillip and I bought a home in a subdivision on a wooded acre lot. It was close to the downtown area of Woodstock, a charming town we adore. It's close to the interstate for him to get to work, and my commute was down to eighteen miles. We dedicated a room for our granddaughter, Madeliyne, who visits twice a month. We have a guest room, I have an art studio, and Phillip has not only a garage and workshop but also a man cave.

I nested for about six months until I felt settled, decorating, making the house our home. The town has excellent restaurants, a yoga studio, craft shows, an amphitheater where they put on free summer concerts, and a wonderful independent bookstore, Fox Tale. It's a beautiful place to live. We were delighted with this move.

When I was in high school, I took an art class and discovered that I like to paint. I enjoy the freedom to create whatever I want with the colors before me. I was proud of what I was able to put on the canvas, as it was a part of me that I was sharing with the world. Then I was told by the art teacher that even with practice, I wouldn't be good enough. So, I quit painting. It was over twenty-five years before I picked up another paintbrush. That's how creativity is squashed, by allowing things that parents, teachers, or friends said to me to shut down my creative process. That art teacher was wrong. I am creative — we all are.

I had been looking for ways for me to be more creative. In town, I found a cute little painting class that I was attending twice a week, where we worked with acrylic paints and would complete a canvas in two or three hours. I would go to the Mexican restaurant for dinner and then to the painting class. I went to a session at least twice a week for a year or so.

Looking back, I don't think I actually went to learn anything, even though I did. I was mixing colors, shading, drawing out the primary forms, devising a plan of action on how I would cover the canvas. The class helped me get my creative juices flowing. More importantly, I needed a safe place to build my confidence as a creative being, and this helped me feel self-assured in my art.

After about a year, I started to paint in the studio with Madeliyne. It's one of her favorite things for us to do. She picks the colors she wants, and I help her with learning the different strokes and brush types so Madeliyne can create what she wants.

I believe we're all creative beings, and it's part of our human nature. I needed to find ways to let out my creativity, as it's also a way I authentically connect with Spirit as well as with others. I take the time to express myself through some artistic medium, and it brings great joy into my life.

After the year of painting, I joined the local yoga studio. I wanted to get some exercise in, and the classes were welcoming for first-timers. I had not participated in any form of yoga, so I tried a bit of everything they offered: hot yoga, ashtanga, Hatha, yin yoga, and vinyasa. Each one had things I enjoyed, and each one had aspects I disliked. But I went to class faithfully two or three times a week for about a year. In this time, I become more flexible, but more importantly, I finally learned to quiet my mind.

My mind is going all the time. I didn't think I could shut it off. Even as I try to drift off to sleep, ideas, thoughts, and things I have to do are always coming up. I had attempted meditation on and off for several years with little success. Oprah Winfrey and Deepak Chopra started a twenty-one-day meditation series in 2013. I have participated in every twenty-one-day meditation series they put out since its introduction. But I continually struggled with quieting the mind. I would say the mantras, and yet my mind always drifted and was making to-do lists rather than being calm and meditating. I fought this for over a year, then yoga happened.

At the end of yoga class, there is about a five- to ten-minute time of Shavasana, or corpse pose, where I relax at the end of the session. Now, after an hour of Ashtanga or Vinyasa yoga, I'm tired. I enjoy the time at the end, where I allow my body to relax and breathe in counts of five. Breathe in and count to five and then exhale to the count of five. By doing this, I was able to finally quiet my mind. At first, I thought it was a fluke, but then I was able to quiet my mind just by doing the breathwork.

It took me over two years before I could meditate daily. I wanted to, but I had to overcome obstacles within myself to accomplish this goal. First, I set the intention to meditate daily, but I had focus issues. I had to work on being able to quiet my mind so I could focus. Once I accomplished that step, I added meditation to my calendar because if it's on my schedule, I tend to do it. This entire process was frustrating, but I focused on each incremental step, not the end result. Now, I would never begin my day without first mediating.

Being able to quiet my mind allowed me to be. I was able to keep my egoic mind at bay for a bit. As time went on, I was able to quiet my mind whenever I wanted to. This ability now gave me control over my reactions to others. I was able to separate what I truly was feeling from how I was reacting to a situation. It gave me pure clarity of thought for the first time.

What I mean by this is that my true self, my soul, was able to speak, and I was able to hear it over the screams of the ego. That still small voice, the whisper in the dark, the heart speaks, was something I could not only hear, but I was able to access it whenever I wanted, as long as I got quiet.

I believe we all have this capability. It's how I communicate with Spirit instead of my ego, pleading with God for something I desire. Real communication is two ways; I ask, and I receive a response. I think when I was asking God all the why questions when I was younger, I never stayed quiet enough to receive a reply. I think if I did, I would have come into myself a lot sooner.

Now, every morning, I begin my day with meditation. Ten minutes each morning allows me to get centered and know all is well, no matter what the day may bring. The few times I have not meditated, I have noticed a difference in how I react to the day's events. I'm not as calm, my egoic mind quickly takes over, and I become less aware of what is going on around me. I am not fully present.

Phillip has noticed the change in me as well. I am much calmer, and things don't seem to faze me. I am peaceful. I'm not stressed, nor do I get upset about too many things. The reason I think this is happening is that I am centered every morning, and I know that all is well.

I get bombarded with all kinds of thoughts and ideas from my ego that are meaningless to my life. Thoughts about what my boss thinks of my work or the comments friends make about an opinion I shared. These notions and feelings keep me from being aware of what my current situation is. Awareness is the discernment of the current state; it's being fully conscious of the present moment.

I remember when I was little, at a cookout with my parents before their divorce, and there were fresh strawberries. It was the first time that Tammi and I ate them. I recall the delightfully sweet taste of that pretty red flesh. I was conscious of the strawberry juice dripping down my chin. That day, I was fully present and thoroughly enjoying every one of the berries. This memory is a perfect example of how to be fully present and in the moment.

When I become fully conscious of the situation or its cause, I can begin to alter my responses to facilitate the changes I want to see in my life. I first had to become aware that there was an issue as I was the one responding negatively. It was my responsibility to change how I was responding to the situation I found myself in; no one else was to blame for my reaction.

Being aware is part of the joy I have in living life. This consciousness is where I realize that I have more happy moments in my life than troubled times. I realized that since Phillip made me feel safe, that when we went camping with the boys, I was utterly enjoying the time together. I wasn't worried about anything. Awareness is how I choose to be happy moment by moment. It's allowing the good to emerge as I am living my ordinary life. For example, I am now aware and enjoying the smell of cookies baking in the oven or the warmth of holding hands while driving with Phillip to run an errand.

Every morning I need to ground myself into the present moment. By doing this, I can begin the day with serenity and peace. I do this through a variety of means, including meditation, prayer, and journaling. By taking this time as I start each day, I have the opportunity to remind myself that each moment I have a choice of how I will proceed. I can pick my attitude. I can alter my emotional state. I can choose to see the best in every situation. I can see both sides of a position and consciously move forward in a calm way toward what I desire.

I need to accept the current situation for what it is. Learning to be thankful for my current state changes the focus from lack to having enough. This gratitude is essential on a universal perspective. My acceptance of what is has allowed peace to enter my life instead of feeling that I am fighting to get by.

For the past several years, I have created a Happiness Project, based on Gretchen Rubin's book of the same name. Recently I had a month where I focused on peace. I want to breathe in calmness each morning so that my day is peaceful. I believe we all have peace inside us, and I wanted to be able to bring peace into my life every day.

The first thing I had to do was slow down. When I was sitting at the stoplight on my way into work, I would look and see the glorious sunrise or admire the distinctive skyline as I crested the hill. Each day I'm given ample opportunities to be in awe of the beautiful world around me. Still, I needed to slow down and take notice.

I needed to be fully in the present moment. Not mulling over the past or worried about the future — these are peace killers and only cause me undue stress. Slowing down reduces the fear in my life as I consciously refocus my attention on what is truly important.

When I slow down, I get clarity. Only when I'm mindful and in the present moment can I unclutter my egoic mind full of thoughts. As I get clear on what I want and define my goals, I can then make clear and decisive decisions on how to move forward.

Holding onto the past does not allow us to live in the present. And peace only occurs in the now. It's old material possessions I hold onto, like the boxes of new Tupperware I have left from selling it over fifteen years ago. Or negative memories that keep me in the past. The only way forward is to let them go.

Releasing the memories, hurt feelings, and pain first requires that I take responsibility for my current situation. I made decisions and choices that got me to this place in life, and if I blame others, I have given up my power to change and, therefore, my ability to regain my peace.

Once I take responsibility, I'm empowered to consciously choose to change my mindset so that I can begin to attract the harmony I want in my life. Peace is a positive state of being. This idea means that I have to choose to feel happy. Feelings are not thrust upon me by others, and I can decide how I feel. No one makes me angry. I decided to get mad at them for something they did. I could've easily chosen to believe that they were being senseless and forgiven them. Why give them the power to take away my peace? No one on this planet can take away my peace unless I give it to them, and why would I choose to give up my peace of mind?

When I decided to be myself and not be concerned with others' opinions of me, peace engulfed me. Peace is a gift from the Divine. When I'm genuinely myself, the Divine within me unites with the Universe. That connection is part of my real state of being. Peace is a part of my daily life if I allow it.

The egoic voice is the one that tries to take away my internal Divine peace. When I started taking yoga, it helped my meditation practice, and I was able to turn off the babbling of my ego. When I wrote in my journal about this, I realized how much peace I felt day in and day out despite the routine daily tasks and annoyances that occur. I also realized that peace had always been there. I just wasn't focused on it. I was choosing to focus on the stress and anxiety I was creating.

Part of acceptance is gratitude for everything I have, which includes any hardships as they're there for me to learn something. The fastest way through the adversity was to ask the Universe, what lesson am I to glean from the experience? Then, I have to get quiet and discern how this situation can teach me something about myself or how I relate to the world around me.

One of the best ways that helped me see all the good in my life was a gratitude journal. It's easy to write down a few items each evening that happened during my day, showing my gratitude. They were things like the beautiful sunrise I witnessed while driving into work or my son passing his math test even though he struggled with the homework. Every day there are things in my life to be appreciative of, and this is where I need to focus my attention to shape the vision I have for my future.

By taking the time to ground myself each day, I started taking the time to learn who I am — my authentic self. I began discovering what I liked instead of what my parents wanted. I was learning about my dreams for my life. The quiet time is how I connect to the Divine as well as to the Divine within me. Only when I get quiet can I hear my soul speaking. In this silence, I uncover the ability to accept myself as I am. This discovery is the ultimate spiritual awakening, loving myself.

I was becoming aware of the thoughts I was thinking. I separated myself from the beliefs and judgments of the situation. Once I was able to do this, I could see the circumstances themselves are always neutral.

I'm the one that blamed myself for the circumstances. Who chose to feel shameful? I did. I imposed those conclusions and emotions about what was happening in my life. No one else did this. It was me. I am responsible. When I stepped outside of myself, I could look at the whole and truly see the conditions.

The hamster wheel of beliefs that kept my mind full of thoughts wasn't necessary. Instead, I can be aware of the situation and consciously choose how to create a better position that has positive outcomes for my family and me. This switch is being mindful—intentionally creating the life I want.

When I became aware of the ego in me, it meant that I was now the observer and, therefore, the agent to change my reactions to the situations I find myself. I have choices in every circumstance: a positive one and a negative one, an opportunity to love, or a decision to fear.

Becoming attentive allows me to grow as a human being. It enables me to expand my horizons. To create a new reality for me to explore, to savor each moment as it occurs. Growth is exploring those parts of me that I have put aside, like the creative teenager who loved to paint.

Awareness is the birthplace of possibility. Everything I want to do, everything I want to start, comes from being aware. To be a successful visionary, I must be as mindful as possible. At every moment, many paths lead forward. Mindfulness helps to tell me the right one to take.

I realized that I had feelings and attachments to the past. The past was hard to let go of, and it affected me emotionally. Yet I have a choice to make, an option to choose a different outlook, a growth mindset instead of a fixed mindset.

The fixed mindset is the idea that I believe my attributes and abilities are inherently static and can't be changed. For example, I thought that I was as smart as I'd ever be. Therefore, that thought process caused me not to try to learn new things. Since I didn't believe my intelligence could change with time and experience, then I couldn't have changed, and my future would have been the same.

A growth mindset is an exact opposite. What I now believe is that my abilities can be cultivated and are malleable. The growth mindset allows me to grow with enthusiasm, time, and a commitment to improving, learning, and become more significant than before. With a growth mindset, failures are short-term setbacks, and the process is usually more important than the outcome. So, with a growth mindset, my future is never predetermined.

I now know, no matter what life throws at me, I will make it through to the other side. I now need to focus on my reactions to life. Was I reacting or responding to the situations? I felt like I was always on alert to put out the fires around me. This feeling is the ego trying to protect me. I realized that I was reacting to life and not responding. Reacting means that I quickly reply to a stimulus. Emotions cause my reactions. When I respond, on the other hand, it means I take a deep breath, become aware, think about the situation, and calmly address the circumstances. See the difference? Reacting leads to more reactions, but only responding can lead to a solution. Knowing myself meant that I could begin responding to life through awareness.

There are many ways to overcome life's hurdles; I need to be open to them as well as actively looking for ways to get past them and move forward. Awareness of the vision helps me to move forward through those times I don't enjoy.

Do I let circumstances dictate my decisions? Are other people's opinions more important than my gut feeling? When I was doing reaction, I wasn't allowing my innate knowledge to flow. I was allowing others to influence my life. As I became more aware of my responses and looked for ways to overcome the hurdles I encountered, I learned to trust my instincts.

My intuition, the gut feeling, is my authentic self that is still connected to the Divine trying to speak to me. When I choose to listen, I tend to have a better life experience as I am following my internal guide. But if I disregard the feeling, I'm ignoring my true self and allowing outside influences to steer my life.

These forces that I allowed to interfere with what I wanted, or thought was best for me, were loved ones saying that they were looking out for me, like Vicki and my mother. Mostly it was my ego trying to instill more fear into my life so I wouldn't move forward. Whatever the outside influences are, I need to be aware that they may not be supportive of me.

There's no limit to what I can change because awareness brings light to every aspect of life. If I constrict my consciousness, everything else will be restricted, too. On the other hand, if I am in a state of expanded awareness, everything else will expand. There is no greater power of transformation than mindfulness. When I am aware, then expansion is unlimited, and the possibilities are endless.

My life happens at this instant in time. The past is gone, and the future is what I create by the choices I make today. I cannot add peace to the past, and I cannot propel it into my future—peace happens at this present moment. For more on being present, I recommend Eckhart Tolle's excellent book, *The Power of Now*.

When I am present, I am fully conscious and aware of what is happening at this moment in time that I find myself. I'm not mulling over the conversation I had yesterday, in the past, with my boss. Nor am I worried about the meeting I'm having later this week, in the future. This moment, I am typing and only thinking about writing this book to help you find peace based on what has worked for me. This moment, you are reading this memoir (thank you!) and learning simple methods that you can apply to fill your life with peace. The present is here, in the now, fully aware and conscious. My authentic self emerges when I make a conscious decision to be myself. Not what others want me to be, not what others expect me to be, but what I am, my genuine self.

When I was going through the aftermath of my trauma, it was hard to look at things from a different perspective. Yet when I did, relief came. The healing process is multifaceted and can take time, especially since it took me so long to take responsibility for my current actions and responses. This act was the first step to reclaiming my power.

As many women know, sexual abuse occurs in one out of three of us by the time we are eighteen years old. It's a disturbing and staggering statistic, and it indicates to me that the amount of personal suffering around me is significant. This suffering shows how the actions of others disempower so many of us. It also suggests that many of us still allow the trauma to make us feel helpless and incapable of overcoming our situation.

Although the healthcare community wants to help us, unlike me, many don't ever get any form of treatment. The few of us that do are woefully underserved due to our fear of disclosing the truth, usually about a loved one. Therefore, I grew up with unresolved issues that still needed addressing long into adulthood. It takes strength to reach out for help. I'm not the victimized child anymore. I'm a survivor who isn't alone, and asking for guidance from Spirit and others I trust in my healing process is an act of empowerment.

Empowerment is the reward of successful action. Doing and power go together since, without the ability to sustain my vision through difficulties and resistance, my dream or goals will wither away. This action isn't ego empowerment, which is driven by the demands of me and mine, which disguise the underlying fear.

Here are the ways I felt when I reacted to life from a fear-based perspective:

- The voices of those around me overly influenced me because I didn't trust myself.

- I was always exhausted from most work I tried to do, and I had trouble sleeping.

- I would pick and choose which parts of the circumstances to respond to; the rest was denied or ignored.

- I was full of doubt and inner turmoil.

Personal empowerment meant that I developed confidence and strength to overcome and live authentically. I felt empowered and at peace once I had taken responsibility for my actions. Here is how peace felt:

- I felt centered.

- I was rested and alert at the same time.

- I was entuned to my emotional state and was authentically me.

- I felt attuned to the situation around me and was aware.

- I noticed signs of confusion and conflict in myself and confronted them head-on.

Reclaiming my power was a process. I needed a bit of courage to move out of my comfort zone, which I received from trusted people, and I was persistent.

The first step was to create boundaries about how I told my story. Not everyone needs to know what suffering I endured. I get to determine whom I share my narrative with and when they get to learn more about me. How much I share was also entirely up to me. Asserting boundaries by letting them know that I don't want to share details was a form of good self-care. For most people, the details of the trauma aren't necessary for empathy and compassion to be shown. And, even if they were family didn't mean I needed to tell them unless I wanted to share the story with them.

Owning the right to how my story unfolds from my perspective isn't about shame or blame. It's about showing my strength and empowerment. As time passed, I gained perspective. I realized that I'm no longer a child, and I can respond differently as an adult to my childhood suffering.

Time allows growth and perspective. As I moved from each phase of life to another, I gained a perception of my development. When I met Phillip, I entered a place of safety. Through scouting and the biker gang, I learned that I belong, and others care about me just as I am. I also gained self-esteem as I grew to know my authentic self and the unique talents that I have. I can see that I've made strides in overcoming past suffering. But other times, negative thoughts invade my thinking and keep me in the past pain. This negative thinking is where I have to be compassionate to myself. I have to speak to myself like I would a loved one: that it's okay to be human. Although the suffering is an event that took place in my past, the essence of trauma is the residual impact it leaves behind on my emotional system.

It's normal to feel that "I should be over this by now; it happened a long time ago." This line of thinking is where I needed to combat shame and understand that the emotional impact of trauma inflicted upon me wasn't my fault. Therefore, however long it takes me to overcome is how long it takes. Allowing shame to come in only keeps me trapped in the past. I must focus on the present moment and be aware that I can choose to feel better.

I had a lengthy discussion concerning the ego with a fellow sexual abuse sufferer. She viewed her ego as a protector that has kept her alive. This woman saw herself as a victim, ashamed that the rape occurred, and still suffering a half a century after the incident. A successful woman in her chosen career, happy in her marriage of over thirty-five years — you would assume she had it all. Yet, she has lived every day since she was raped in a state of trepidation.

I, on the other hand, see the ego as the voice that kept me locked in a room, too fearful of ever wanting to leave. I now see myself as a survivor, proud that I have overcome the fear and feeling that I can help others to do the same. I'm successful professionally and happily married for over twenty years. I chose to take back my power and not live in a state of fear.

Perspective is astonishing. One view kept this woman locked in living a troubled life, while my viewpoint lets me become my authentic self. I learned that day that mindsets play a significant role in determining the realization of my dreams and my ability to overcome them. My egoic mind is always a negative influence. Its job is to instill fear. But I learned to master the destructive force of this instinctual mechanism that does more harm than good.

My ego believed it was separate from everything, and I existed outside of the community, which wasn't correct. My body was the ego's proof that I'm distinct from others. Therefore, if I'm detached, then I'm isolated. Thus, I needed to be more concerned with self-preservation than with the good of others. This idea is where the "us versus them" mentality arises.

My ego's perception was inaccurate. My egoic mind took everything personally. It was full of drama, always wanting more than it had. Comparing and complaining was a way for my ego to strengthen itself. My egoic mind is the loveless mind which seeks suffering. Misery was the narrative of my ego. It's how it kept my authentic self at bay.

I underestimated the ruthlessness of my ego to keep me in a state of suffering, in which I voluntarily participated by the choices I made based on fear. Anxiety was my ego, saying that I hadn't been here before; therefore, it needs to take charge of the situation. It did this by creating different types of fear to maintain control, to keep me small, and to stop me from achieving my dreams.

As a self-conscious emotion, shame was the feeling that kept me feeling inadequate or unworthy, which was a lie of the ego. Although another person can trigger shame in me, I'm responsible for this self-inflicted state of negativity. Yet, I hid this sting from others so they couldn't see. I perceived my self-consciousness and vulnerability as weaknesses.

However, for a wound to heal, it must first be exposed. My egoic mind doesn't want me to heal. The ego wants me to believe that revealing the injuries to the light will cause me additional harm. Again, this is a lie.

The ego wanted me to be stuck in my fear, so it used defense mechanisms to numb me so that I wouldn't look for a solution. It repressed my memories of past events as a way to protect me from the trauma. I became very controlling to keep me safe from chaos. I blamed others so that I didn't take responsibility for my actions and therefore kept me stuck playing the victim. By doing all of these things, it kept me from facing the need to heal. Healing of a wound can be uncomfortable, but I needed to release the shame of the past and become my authentic self.

Blame strengthened my ego. Culpability is a self-defense mechanism, which allowed my ego to keep my self-esteem intact. It's easier to avoid responsibility for a problem if I can deflect the obligation to another person. There's a difference in searching for the reason for a situation and trying to place blame. One is constructive and helpful, while the other is destructive.

My ego always thought it was right all the time. Therefore, it used judgment, another form of blame, to keep me locked in negative patterns of behavior. Since my egoic mind believes it's separate from others, it also thinks it is okay to judge them. But, others are a mirror of myself, and when I judge others, I ultimately judge myself. I see this reflection when my ego overreacts to those things I'm not willing to change in myself.

The ego believes there's power in judgment. It thinks, therefore, that when I judge another, I'm more powerful than the other is, which is false. My ego equated supremacy and judgment with strength and control. This belief, of course, is another lie. The real power comes from knowing my authentic self and living from that place of honesty.

Loss aversion was a strong motivator for me, even if the potential gains outweighed the possible losses. I became attached to things and individuals. I grew attached to my possessions—things like my job, my position, my lifestyle, etcetera. To chase a dream would mean I'd have to give something up. Because of this fear of loss, I chose to put things on hold.

When I allowed fear to interfere with my decision making, I chose to do nothing, which is still a choice. This choice to do nothing kept me from my dreams. If I'm only concerned about maintaining my current status, then I can never move forward. So, when facing a decision, I need to ask myself, what's the worst thing that could happen? If I can live with that outcome, I will decide to move forward.

Fear of loss is a crucial way my ego kept me from growing into my full potential. What I needed in the past may not be what I need in the present or the future. My authentic self is better at determining how to follow my dreams than my ego, who wants to maintain the norm.

Moving into the unknown is scary. But, being concerned about what others think about me or my abilities is my ego exerting itself by trying to keep me from exploring new things. Missing the mark, but still experiencing growth, isn't failing. If I learn, then I didn't fail.

My ego wants me to maintain the current standard of my life. Nothing new or different, as that may have an unexpected outcome, and I need to avoid the unknown. This unfamiliar setting means that my dreams are outside the acceptable norm. My ego will do its best to keep me from attaining those goals, as there are risks involved.

The Universe wanted me to stretch and reach for my dreams by creating a path I haven't been on before. To accomplish this, I needed to overcome the fear of failure and learn to move out of my comfort zone. When I'm on the right path, and stress builds up, I know that my ego has returned to keep my life ordinary.

CHAPTER 7 DISCOVERING WHO YOU AUTHENTICALLY ARE

MY CHOICES TODAY GOVERN TOMORROW

Raven transcended the fear within;

Realizing that she always had the love

Within her, she craved.

As an adult, I feel that I have experienced enough of life to see that one constant is change. I grow, circumstances transform, people develop. All of this is observable; therefore, if everybody changes, then the past can't be a good indication of the future.

Even those around me who don't seem to have the desire to grow still change. Based on the circumstances that occur in their lives and by the choices that they make, friends, and family change. Even when I don't make a decision, I'm still choosing, which has an impact on my life that doesn't allow things to stay the same. Thus, despite whether I grow or not, the future will be different from the past.

As I grow and develop, how I perceive the past can be altered and reframed. I learn from the past and determine ways to prevent unwanted situations. I make informed decisions and take responsibility for my choices so I can move forward in the direction of my goals and dreams. In this way, I am validating that I am creating a better future than my past.

As I have learned, to make my future better than my past, I have to believe that it's possible. Achieving this belief may take a bit of courage, as I work to overcome my fears and move towards a growth mindset.

When I had a fixed mindset, I would latch onto the disappointment as more proof that I wasn't enough. Here again, I didn't do it right, so why bother trying another time? I used the past as evidence that I would repeat the mistake. Of course, if I don't learn from the misstep, then I will be entirely correct. Learning from the past is how I can make changes so that my future outcomes are more like what I want.

Choosing to learn from my mistake moves me away from a fixed mindset into a growth mindset. And my recovery from failure becomes much faster. Now I analyze the situation, and I make a conscious decision to learn from it. What went right, what went wrong, how can I improve? By asking myself these questions, I'm able to bounce back from frustration more quickly because I know I can. I am enough, and I have shown myself over time that I am resilient, and I can move out of my comfort zone.

A few years back, I took an online course by Brené Brown based on her book *The Gifts of Imperfection*. In this course, the goal was to help bolster my self-esteem and personal development. One of the exercises is to write, "I am enough" on our hand in the morning and look at it throughout the day to remind ourselves of our inherent worthiness.

Through the course, I remembered that I'm an eternal being, and I am limitless. My true self is pure love personified. Therefore, my journey towards living my life isn't about searching for anything outside of myself. It's about discovering the love that's already within me and expressing it in all of my relationships.

The recognition that I'm pure love is evidence that I'm enough. My creation by a Divine source is tangible evidence that I'm worthy, and I'm good enough just the way I am. The hard part for me is believing this timeless truth.

The ego's been yelling at me about my unworthiness for most of my life. It takes a conscious effort on my part to alter my thinking patterns. From an evidence-based scenario, I can see that, over time, I've had successes. I was able to learn to feel safe, even if I was alone. I made friends, and they care for me just as I am. I can help groups and individuals grow and have fun. I have overcome some fears. Changing my perspective wasn't easy. It was something I accomplished over time, and there are still days I have to work on it.

Since there is evidence, I remind myself that I'm good enough just as I am right now. Yes, I have made errors, but since I have learned from them, the growth mindset shows that I have overcome that mistake. I have changed my perspective; therefore, the past doesn't determine my future. My choices today govern tomorrow.

The day I decided I was good enough was the day I set myself free. Free from the negative tape recordings, the ego tries to replay. Free from the expectations I take on or impose upon myself. Free from the limited mindset, which can't learn from the mistakes made.

I had judged myself out of my natural state — I can only be who I am, and it's good enough. I'm worthy just as I am. When I do my best as I move forward in life, taking risks, learning as I go, my authentic self emerges and thrives. Again, I see the proof that I'm good enough and worthy just by being authentically me.

We're all born unique individuals. Even identical twins have distinct personalities. Since we all arrive on this planet as separate entities, why do we try so hard to fit into society? Why do we want to be "normal"? Why is our uniqueness a cause of fear, so much so that we want to hide away our authentic selves?

I spent the first ten years of my life being unique and authentic, then the next ten years trying to fit in, somewhere along the way, who I genuinely am got lost. As my ego instilled fear, I started to believe that I needed to wear masks to be accepted. I no longer wear disguises that hide my authentic self from others, or the armor of perfectionism to hide my flaws, but instead ask for help when I need it. Yet, I wanted others to be who they are, to be authentic, and their unique selves. What a paradox we live.

I turned fifty years old last November. Before the big party, my son gave me; I decided I was no longer going to dye my hair to hide the gray, which I had been doing for about fifteen years. When my sister, a former hairdresser, arrived, she wanted to spray my hair to cover the gray hair and was disappointed when I wouldn't let her. I told her my authentic self has gray hair, and I was allowing it to grow out.

Over the past year, I have had many compliments on my hair; it has been overwhelming. Perfect strangers have come up to me to admire my hair. Several members of my book club have discussed how brave I am for going natural. Just last week at a dinner event, a man I had never met before went out of his way to tell me how stunning my hair was. Being true to who I am is beautiful, and other people notice it.

I was making my own choice and risked scorn from family and co-workers, but only heard that my hair seemed healthier than it was before and that I was becoming more myself. I did this for me — and it didn't hurt that I was saving almost $1,000 year on getting my hair colored at the salon. In choosing to be my genuine self, I became more beautiful to myself and others. I risked being different and instead found authentic connections.

My goal is to be a contradiction in the world. To be at peace, when there is turmoil all around me. I want my reaction to all things to be a loving response, not one of fear. I am choosing to be different and encouraging others to be their unique selves.

If I want others to be their authentic selves, then I need to reciprocate and be my unique self as well. This interchange is the only way to be true to my beliefs and my soul. In doing this, I weed out those people in my life who prefer the masks that I used to wear.

Once I was able to accept my differences, the unique parts of myself, my weirdness, then I was ready to let go of the fear and understand that I am one of a kind. I'm a fantastic individual. If I'm hiding behind the armor and masks that the ego said were needed to be accepted, then no one else will see how wonderful I am.

We are all different. But we don't have to be afraid of our differences — no need for comparison. Beauty is within each of us; it's part of the differences we see in one another. Being the same, fitting in, being ordinary is boring. Who wants to be boring? Not me.

So, being different and not fitting in isn't a negative thing, after all. I was born to stand out, not blend in, as I am a unique individual. Choosing to be okay with not fitting in was a step in maintaining my authenticity with others and being happy with myself.

Being fully present allows my authentic self to emerge as the ego evaporates. Only in the present moment can I be me. Why? Because the past and the future are projections of the ego. Remember that the ego is the labeling mechanism. The ego determines what is safe and what "normal" is. But right now, in this minute, the ego doesn't exert itself. My authentic self occupies the present.

By fully participating at this moment in time, my authentic self takes over. That is why when I'm alone or in the flow of creativity, magic happens. My true self is in control when time passes, and I don't realize it. This state is a natural state for human beings. Yet, many people rarely experience this magical state of awareness.

Being fully present is where our strength comes. It's the time where I'm my toughest. It's when I have no fear and am confident. My resilience comes forth, love is the only response, and peace exists. At this moment, all is well with my soul, and I'm happy just the way I am. I'm not trying to fit in; I'm just being.

Brené Brown writes that the only way humans can genuinely connect is to embrace vulnerability. I needed to recognize that my weaknesses are part of my authentic self. I can't be authentic with others unless I'm honest and share all of who I am, and that includes my vulnerabilities.

Conventionally, vulnerability is seen as a weakness. The idea of being exposed — defects, inadequacies, mistakes, and all — is, for most people, totally petrifying. My ego was trying to protect me from being exposed. I used to think, if I don't tell people my story of trauma, then they won't see me as weak. But as Brené Brown has shown through her research, being vulnerable isn't a liability — it's an asset. Enduring trauma is an asset, as I am a survivor. Being vulnerable is my ability to allow people to see that I'm not perfect, I make mistakes, and I don't have all the answers. It's letting people know that I'm human; that I'm just like them.

Vulnerability is courageously showing my true self, which can feel uncomfortable. But I push past the discomfort. As an alternative to the armor, I now clothe myself in garments that allow me to connect — those made of empathy, compassion, humbleness, kindness, patience, and forgiveness, topped with love. By doing so, I open the door to more imagination, invention, and more authentic connections with others, which is more than worth the effort.

So, I began to surround myself with people who remind me

more about my future than my past. I want people who are encouraging, the people who are excited for me to try new ventures or take a class. Monica and Joni show me that no matter what your age, you can still learn and grow. Carolyn helps me to see the humor in myself and all areas of life. Mike reminds me that passion comes in all varieties and that all are needed. Robin encourages me to reach outside my comfort zone so that I can achieve my dreams. Hyphen reminds me to take all that life throws at me in stride, but to always stand up for my beliefs. These are my real friends, the ones who look at my best attributes and speak in a positive way to me. They remind me of the successes I've had, as a way to inspire me to keep moving forward. I make new friends in the areas where I am growing. It can be helpful to have someone learning with me to discuss and problem-solve together.

Releasing those people from my life that have a negative influence on me is an essential step to safeguarding that my future doesn't resemble my past. By ensuring that I have people who are positive and encouraging around, I help myself enlarge the possibilities of a better future.

My growth and development didn't happen overnight. I wanted things to happen as fast as possible, as I am impatient with myself. It took time, thirty-five years total, because I had a long journey to take. I made small steps as I moved forward. But I needed to be kind to myself, give a little self-care and self-love. I had to pay attention to the incremental steps I took as I grew.

Belief is paramount to being able to do anything. I had to have confidence in my abilities, the conviction to move forward, and faith that my dreams would become my reality. Maintaining this belief is essential, which is why I needed to take pride in my victories along the way. Every disappointment that I overcame, each circumstance I seized, and the individuals who arrived along the way that I recognized were there to help me. All the success along the way helped me maintain my belief that the future would be better than my past because I am creating it every day.

Being conscious and aware of what is happening in my life helped me to move toward the desires of my hearts. Fully being in the present moment allowed me to see the synchronicities in my life and respond to them in a way that kept me going in the right direction. When I needed to serve others, the opportunity came with scouting and the biker gang. When I decided to build a website, a free online class appeared in my email before I began any research. When I wanted to join a writer's group, I saw one was meeting at the local library. By living a conscious lifestyle, I can stitch these moments together to see that the Universe is assisting me in some way. The Universe gives me bits of information to show me I'm on the right path or that I need to alter my mindset.

As I began to walk toward positive change in my life, the Universe, that Divine energy, took even more steps toward me. These are the synchronicities that began to appear in my life. New experiences and amazing possibilities started to open all around me. These synchronicities are a source of joy and wonder in my life. Still, I must become aware of them as they occur. It's rooted in taking my intention and creating a result. If I have a problem, I plan to solve it. So, I review the issue and evaluate potential solutions. But most of the time, a simple answer doesn't exist, and I have to create a resolution.

Creating, or creativity is a magical key to generate more synchronous moments in my life. When I'm creative, I'm in sync and in the flow with the universal power. In other words, I'm inspired. The word inspiration means "in the Spirit." I get these inspirational moments of creativity without the cause and effect I expect from my logical mind. It just hits me, and this synchronicity operates at the deeper level of my awareness. It doesn't come from my conscious, rational brain. In spiritual terms, synchronicity is the ultimate ability to connect my needs with an answer from my soul.

I became open and receptive to what was happening in the present moment. I became humble. I learned to recognize the disguises that the ego used to keep me small. Anxiety about the future, depression from the past, anger at being dismissed, and doubt about making a choice are ways the ego kept me from growth. My imperfections are part of my uniqueness. To be authentically me, I have to know my faults. I shouldn't fear my vulnerabilities, as they have no power, but I should be humble if my limitations are exposed. I'm the perfect and only rendition of me that exists, despite my flaws.

I found and am living my passion, which is to help others overcome their fears. By sharing my story in this book, through the weekly blog posts on my website, and coaching individuals, helping people to overcome is my goal in life. Following it was initially daunting, but it's as simplistic as doing something I love. It's not about changing my life in one day; it's about adding more joy to each day that I live. The more passion I have, the more inclined I am to work hard on self-improvement, thus increasing my chances of success.

By having a growth mindset, I opened up to countless possibilities that could arise. Furthermore, I notice opportunities in a different light. The light of personal development and that never-ending potential allows me to shine in new and inconceivable ways as I apply my new knowledge.

My passion makes the impossible possible. My brain's wired so that when my soul ignites, I no longer flinch when I come upon obstacles that appear in my way. I can imagine the possibilities and the opportunities for progress. In contrast, when I was dispassionate, I only saw the roadblocks and the reasons why the dream or the goal was out of reach. Passion reinforces my determination to overcome the obstacles I encounter, and I become more resilient.

I journaled my intentions. Writing down my dreams helped me to focus my purpose and my ability to receive the synchronous outcomes I desire. The act of writing can force me to organize my thoughts and make concrete the emotional turbulence swirling around in my head.

When I was in therapy, I was instructed to journal. I've had an on-again-off-again relationship with my journal since high school. At first, I did much writing in my journal as a way to deal with anger and other emotions I didn't understand. Then my journal was read by my sister, and secrets I wasn't ready to reveal came out. Therefore, I quit the journaling practice.

In 2018, I read Julia Cameron's book, *The Artist's Way*, which rekindled my journaling practice. She calls them morning pages, a daily act of releasing that centers us. When I restarted journaling, I didn't realize how much more fulfilling my life would become. When I took the time each day to organize and clarify my thoughts, I began to be more aware and more present in each of the moments of my life. I started to realize that the choices I made last week impacted my results this week. I began to make connections and could consciously choose to improve my life.

I still write three pages every morning as I start my day. In this way, I have the opportunity to be grateful for yesterday, and to look forward to this day's events and the intentions I have for it. I'm purposely setting the attitude for the day as it begins. I am taking responsibility for the activities that are planned for and realizing that those unplanned things don't need to take away my joy.

Writing also accesses the left-brain, the analytical side. While this part of the brain is busy, my right-brain is free to do what it does best — create, discern, and feel. In this way, journaling removed mental blocks and allowed me to use all of my brain to understand the world I live in and myself better.

This journaling practice is also a great way to let go of my attachment to the outcome. I can delve into why I'm not trusting or why I want things in a certain way. Journaling is a safe place to review my mindsets and an easy way to alter them into more productive and positive ways.

One of my favorite quotes about fear comes from Marianne Williamson's book, *A Return to Love*:

> *Our deepest fear is not that we are inadequate. Our deepest fear is that we are powerful beyond measure. It is our light, not our darkness, that most frightens us.*

Once I admit to myself that I'm empowered, and in control, then I'm accountable and bound to that knowledge. I can no longer hide behind rationalizations that I'm not good enough or that I don't know what I want. I'm a phenomenal individual, and I have to be responsible for my reality. Wakening to my responsibility to myself brought forth changes in my life. Reclaiming my responsibility for my life was the way to change the world around me, and that's why it was so daunting.

Being responsible for my life means two things: I have to stop blaming others for what happens to me, and I have to accept the consequences of my actions.

It didn't matter what my mother, or anyone else, ever did to me; I had the responsibility to work through the healing process. Only I could do the necessary work to heal. I also had to keep in mind that blaming myself keeps me from facing the fear that I needed to overcome.

Despite what happened to me, where I am today is because of the consequences of my actions. The way I overcame was to realize that, by taking responsibility, I could now change my story. I became empowered to alter the course I'm on by changing how I responded to the situations I found myself.

Letting go of my fear was a process. This process took a long time because of how stubborn my ego was concerning my frame of mind, and how long I continued to blame others for the issues in my life.

The moment when I was in college that I took responsibility for the choices I made; I altered the course of my life. This choosing to be responsible for my responses in life allowed empowerment to take place. Empowerment enabled me to forgive those who harmed me, as well as to forgive myself for being trapped in despair.

The responsibility I took for myself allowed me to make the changes I wanted to see in my life. As I released the fear, the anger and pain subsided. This falling away from negativity allowed more joy and peace to enter my life. In turn, it enabled me to see the possibilities for a happier life ahead.

Understanding that the past doesn't have to repeat itself is part of my newfound positive outlook on life. The gloom that hung over me lifted, and I started to emerge from the doldrums into the sun. I began to look forward and began to plan for good events to enter my life.

I reached out to others and made friends. I attended events that I enjoyed — explored those things about myself that the ego had hidden away to keep me small. I started to see that good things were happening, and I felt good more days than I felt terrible. Realizing that I was the creator of my future, not the events of the past, I accepted happiness as my new state of normalcy.

Now that I have settled into my new positive outlook on life, I began to recognize that I had some limiting beliefs. I realized that the tapes playing in my head needed throwing out, and a new playlist installed. When events occur that once triggered me, I can now see they are harmless. I am a strong adult who can respond in new ways and can create the life I desire.

In doing so, I realize that everything is achievable if I focus my attention on what I want to create in my life. The positive mindset allows me to reframe the story I told myself. I didn't alter the facts but reminded myself that the events are in the past and don't have a bearing on the present unless I choose to allow it.

Reframing is a tool that I utilize to show the ego that it's no longer in control. I continue this growth mindset with self-directed learning. This education allows me to learn more about myself. This discovery is a lifelong process filled with growth, love, fun, and peace. This place of discovering is where I am currently living. There are still days that I may falter into a place of anxiety, but they are now far and few. And when they occur, I quickly become aware, take a few deep breaths, and I regain my joy and peace.

I have to recognize that I'm not alone. Spirit is always with me if I'm willing to listen. The Divine brings others into my life to help me on my path. I need to learn to recognize these blessings in my life.

The main person Spirit sent to me was Phillip, my husband. He provided me a safe place to begin dealing with the way I reacted to the situations in my life. Later, Philip helped me to reach out to others and spread my wings. Phillip taught me to stand on my own, and even when he wasn't with me to be fearless. Through the years, he has grown with me; having a partner in all aspects of life is a beautiful blessing.

Now I feel bold and fearless as I go through my day-to-day life. I look for the opportunities that Spirit gives me to help and inspire others to live an authentic experience that they love. I know that I'm to assist others in seeing they can overcome their own wounds and traumas.

These are the steps I took, and so can you. You can be the bold and authentic person you are created to be. Your life can be all that you desire; you need to make a choice. It's always been in your power to change, but the ego has tricked you.

Now that the light has been shown into your dark corner, and you know the truth, you can overcome. You can live a life of joy and peace. It's the only choice you have to make. You can elect to remain in fear or choose love. I know you can choose love; I did.

I believe in your ability to overcome. You can take responsibility for your life, which will empower you to see that you can make the change. By doing so, you see that your past isn't an indication of your future and that you can overcome your limiting beliefs through reframing your story. With self-directed growth leading the way, you will begin to discover your authentic self and live the life you always wanted.

This life of joy and peace is our birthright. I came into the world knowing it, but along the way, I forgot. This book is your reminder from Spirit to get back on the right path. To have the ego release its control over you, and to follow your heart.

The first time I followed my heart, it led me to Phillip. That heart decision has brought all of my dreams into reality. I followed my heart, which wasn't easy to do, but I got quiet and listened. I do it every morning through meditation and journaling. It's what keeps my joy and peace grounded in Spirit, so as I go through the day, I'm confident that all is well.

Choose to get quiet and listen to your heart. Trust it, as it's always connected to the Divine. Your heart knows best, as it's authentically you; the Divine being of light and love, full of joy and peace that is to bless the Earth with your presence. Be bold; be you by choosing love. I know you can make the choice.

Afterword

Thank you for witnessing my transformation. There are many lessons I've learned. Some were more difficult than others. In remembering who I was born to be, I also recalled the tremendous spiritual power that allows us to overcome every obstacle in life we will encounter.

I now live my daily life from a place of love. What does this mean? It signifies that I unconditionally accept those I encounter as they are- without judgment. It shows up as a sincere smile, a warm hug, even when they are not their best. It also implies that I am no longer wearing armor or masks to hide my authentic self. You see who I am- the good, the bad, and the parts I am still transforming.

The awareness I now have each day helps my mindset to stay positive. When I am not my best self, I am quick to take responsibility for my mood, missteps, and words. Yes- I've had to dig deep into my shadow self to learn that I am worthy, just as I am for me to learn to love myself. We are all unique. We were all born to be different and stand out. And we must all learn to embrace our authentic selves.

This transformation comes through our compassionate nature to accept others and ourselves by using the magic of the Raven Clan. Humanity's story is one of survival. It's about overcoming our fears and limiting beliefs through acceptance.

Acknowledging our stories allows us to reframe them without shame, blame, or guilt. It recognizes the truth that the soul sees in the light. The ego is what holds us back. It's the reason we stay in fear for so long.

The hero's journey is a simple, intuitive story with a spiritual truth we all know. But our egoic minds try to complicate it. It took reading the many books I recommend to help me unmuddle my mind to see the simplicity of the life lessons they were offering. It's also why I offer this guide for you. When we are presented with another perspective to view our lives, it helps us step back and re-evaluate our perception. It offers us a way to reframe our own stories in ways that inspire us to move past the fear.

So, what is keeping you stuck? Although the ego may keep you fearful, it's doing its job. It wants to protect you from harm. But bruised feelings aren't necessarily harmful when compared to a tiger stalking you. The ego doesn't discern the difference. It just sounds a loud alarm. Our souls can determine the risk if we listen to its whispers.

When we learn the soulful lessons and grow spiritually, it enables us to take flight and soar above the obstacles we face. Through forgiveness of ourselves and others, we heal from past traumas. By accepting the ego's role of protector, we can learn to determine what is indeed harmful and when we can dismiss the ego's alarm.

The significant lesson I hope you see is that all healing, for ourselves and humanity, comes through responding in all situations with unconditional love. Trauma doesn't wane unless love is the salve used to heal the wounds. Hate doesn't melt away unless love is applied to the words and deeds to bring unification. Confidence doesn't arise from within us until we learn to love and accept our authentic selves. Fear doesn't dissipate until we allow love to reframe the stories we tell.

Truth is simplistic to the soul. It knows we come from unconditional love. Our soul knows its purpose is to love unconditionally everyone it meets. The soul looks for ways to unify, not separate, and divide. The egoic mind lies to us to keep us from making authentic and loving connections with others.

Love is a creative force. When we accept the truth and integrate it into our lives, we transform it from a state of fear to a state of grace. From one of division to one of unity. From a state of disconnection to authentic, loving connections. We become enlightened as our shadow selves' darkness lessens as the light of love illuminates our path.

Our souls have always been, and it will always be. Eternal life is the state of our souls. All the love we give and receive is about unity and integration. The soul is all-inclusive, which means that our egos are a part of us; we are to accept and love.

I hope I have caused you to become curious about discovering your authentic self. I want to think my courage to shine the light of love upon my shadow self helps you seek your inner truth.

When we go within, we will always find the answers we seek. The love we look for outside of ourselves, we must first find within us. Then we must take this unconditional love to all we meet.

When we intentionally respond with love in all circumstances, we open ourselves to receiving by being fully present. Seeing through the eyes of love and not fear allows us to respond from the heart and not react from an egoic perspective. This loving perspective guides us to unification with others, and they, too, will see your love for them.

Remember that you are worthy-right now. I love you and accept you just as you are. I know you can overcome your fears and limiting beliefs because it's your spiritual journey like it was mine. To return to love, we all seek by remembering our authentic selves.

Suggested Reading

My growth and development along my journey were enabled by the reading I did, starting with the Holy Bible given to me by my grandmother. Through the words of these authors, I was able to open up my mind, expand, grow, and learn the universal truths that were in their writings.

- *A Return to Love* by Marianne Williamson
- *A Year of Miracles* by Marianne Williamson
- *A Course in Miracles* by Dr. Helen Schucman
- *A Course in Miracles Made Easy* by Alan Cohen
- *The Gifts of Imperfection* by Brene Brown
- *Daring Greatly* by Brene Brown
- *The Alchemist* by Paulo Coelho
- *The Warrior of the Light* By Paulo Coelho
- *The Power of Now* by Eckhart Tolle
- *A New Earth* by Eckhart Tolle
- *The Four Agreements* by Don Miguel Ruiz
- *The Mastery of Love* by Don Miguel Ruiz
- *Jesus: A Story of Enlightenment* by Deepak Chopra
- *Muhammad: A Story of the Last Prophet* by Deepak Chopra
- *Buddha: A Story of Enlightenment* by Deepak Chopra
- *God a Story of Revelation* by Deepak Chopra
- *The Future of God* by Deepak Chopra
- *The 13th Disciple a Spiritual Adventure* by Deepak Chopra

- *You Are the Universe* by Deepak Chopra

- *Power Freedom and Grace* by Deepak Chopra

- *The Book of Secrets* by Deepak Chopra

- *Seven Spiritual Laws of Success* by Deepak Chopra

- *Reinventing the Body, Resurrecting the Soul* by Deepak Chopra

- *Super Genes* by Deepak Chopra

- *Super Brain* by Deepak Chopra

- *MetaHuman* by Deepak Chopra

- *Journey of Souls* by Michale Newton

- *Scared Contracts* by Caroline Myss

- *Anatomy of the Spirit* by Caroline Myss

- *The Secret* by Rhonda Byrne

- *The 5 Minute Motivator: Learn the Secrets to Success, Health, and Happiness* by Dr. Eric Kaplan

- *The Impersonal Life* by Joseph Benner

- *Mary Magdalene Revealed* by Meggan Watterson

- *Wisdom Codes* by Greg Braden

Acknowledgments

Oprah Winfrey, so much of my spiritual growth came through the people, books, ideas that were introduced to me through the Oprah Winfrey Show and the OWN network; including but not limited to Gary Zukav, Marianne Williamson, Wayne Dyer, Eckhart Tolle, Mark Nepo, Brené Brown, Carolyn Myss, Deepak Chopra, Dr. Christine Northrup, Ester Hicks, Elizabeth Gilbert, Iyana Vanzant, Rob Bell, Gabrielle Bernstein, and Gretchen Rubin.   Thank you for your continuing efforts to spread the message that Spirit and love can overcome; if only we are open to it.

Most importantly, my soul mate, Phillip. A true gift from my Heavenly Father who showed me what true love is and that I can be truly safe in this world. Because I felt completely safe in your presence, I was able to take the journey back to my true self. Thank you for your adoring love, your gentleness with me, and for your continual patience. I love you with all my heart.

Other titles from Higher Ground Books & Media:

Wise Up to Rise Up by Rebecca Benston

Forgiven and Not Forgotten by Terra Kern

For His Eyes Only by John Salmon, Ph.D.

Miracles: I Love Them by Forest Godin

32 Days with Christ's Passion by Mark Etter

Knowing Affliction and Doing Recovery by John Baldasare

Out of Darkness by Stephen Bowman

Breaking the Cycle by Willie Deeanjlo White

Healing in God's Power by Yvonne Green

Chronicles of a Spiritual Journey by Stephen Shepherd

The Real Prison Diaries by Judy Frisby

My Name is Sam...And Heaven is Still Shining Through by Joe Siccardi

Add these titles to your collection today!

http://www.highergroundbooksandmedia.com

Do you have a story to tell?

Higher Ground Books & Media is an independent Christian-based publisher specializing in stories of triumph! Our purpose is to empower, inspire, and educate through the sharing of personal experiences.

Please visit our website for our submission guidelines.

http://www.highergroundbooksandmedia.com

Made in the USA
Las Vegas, NV
12 September 2021